Performance Management for Agile Organizations

Tim Baker

Performance Management for Agile Organizations

Overthrowing The Eight Management Myths That Hold Businesses Back

Tim Baker
WINNERS-at-WORK Pty Ltd
Brisbane, Queensland, Australia

ISBN 978-3-319-40152-2   ISBN 978-3-319-40153-9 (eBook)
DOI 10.1007/978-3-319-40153-9

Library of Congress Control Number: 2016957151

© The Editor(s) (if applicable) and The Author(s) 2017
This work is subject to copyright. All rights are solely and exclusively licensed by the Publisher, whether the whole or part of the material is concerned, specifically the rights of translation, reprinting, reuse of illustrations, recitation, broadcasting, reproduction on microfilms or in any other physical way, and transmission or information storage and retrieval, electronic adaptation, computer software, or by similar or dissimilar methodology now known or hereafter developed.
The use of general descriptive names, registered names, trademarks, service marks, etc. in this publication does not imply, even in the absence of a specific statement, that such names are exempt from the relevant protective laws and regulations and therefore free for general use.
The publisher, the authors and the editors are safe to assume that the advice and information in this book are believed to be true and accurate at the date of publication. Neither the publisher nor the authors or the editors give a warranty, express or implied, with respect to the material contained herein or for any errors or omissions that may have been made.

Cover illustration: akindo / Getty

Printed on acid-free paper

This Palgrave Macmillan imprint is published by Springer Nature
The registered company is Springer International Publishing AG
The registered company address is: Gewerbestrasse 11, 6330 Cham, Switzerland

This book is dedicated to Carol May Baker, my wife and life partner. I'm an infinitely better person with her in my life. Carol's unconditional love, unfailing support, and abiding belief in me, sustain me.

Preface

Management as a Profession is Ultra-Conservative

Performance management is a hot topic; it has been for some time. Managers universally want to know what can be done to escalate company performance. *What are the secrets, shortcuts, and strategies? Where do I begin?* Employers and their managers all want answers to these and other performance questions. They want to know what can be done to optimize performance, gain a competitive or adaptive advantage, and build capacity. Further, they want to know how to responsively deal with the fickle and ever-changing demands and heightened standards of the end-user: the customer. Being agile, maneuverable, and flexible are success factors for the modern high-performing company. Where to begin?

Agility—more than ever—is the driver of organizational performance. In an organizational context, agility can be defined as:

> the ability to stay open to new directions and be continually proactive, helping to assess the limits or indeed risks of existing approaches and ensuring that leaders and followers have an agile and change-ready mindset to enable them and ultimately the organization to keep moving, changing, adapting.[1]

The way we evaluate business performance has progressed considerably since the 1950s. Prior to the mid-twentieth century, performance was primarily measured in terms of profit margins; other factors weren't taken into account. To gain perspective, it's helpful to understand the successive schools of thought on evaluating performance and their implication for speed, maneuverability, and flexibility. Each performance movement has its relative benefits and blind spots—they each emerged from deficiencies in previous approaches.

Research suggests a link between an agile enterprise and its performance management practices.[2] The top traits of an agile business, for instance, are a high performance culture, flexibility in management practices and resource allocation, organizational structures supporting collaboration, and rapid decision-making and execution. I discuss these characteristics in detail in *Performance Management for Agile Organizations*.

If agility is critical to organizational success—as it's widely reported—then we need to know precisely what *agility* means—and doesn't mean. What are the characteristics and preconditions of agility in an organizational setting? Although there are myriad definitions and models of organizational agility, there are few, if any, used to actually evaluate business performance. Most agility models describe what the organization needs to do to be flexible, adaptable, and maneuverable. But these models don't consider the dimensions of agility and how they should be assessed. The Organizational Agility model that I have developed promises to fill the gap.

Building on management guru Rosabeth Moss Kanter's original three-pronged model of organizational speed, I add four additional dimensions of agility to make up seven forms of agility. The model offers a comprehensive framework for appraising agility in any workplace setting.

I then examine eight long-standing roadblocks to agility. Each obstacle is based on management myths rooted in Frederick Taylor's scientific management philosophy.

What's commonly referred to as *Taylorism*, began over 100 years ago on the factory assembly lines of several businesses, including the *Ford Motor Company*. Taylor's philosophy was very successful at yielding high profit margins. But work itself has radically transformed from the factory assembly lines of the early twentieth century to the knowledge work of the twenty-first century. Notwithstanding this transformation in the world of work, the thinking and practice of scientific management is still ubiquitous today. Taylorism continues to guide and inform our performance management practices.

What's more, the philosophy of scientific management is deeply embedded in the psyche of management. It's been the driving force for performance practices that are outdated. My claim that management thinking is passé, is tempting to dismiss. The mind-boggling transformation from the birth of the industry suggests performance management practices have advanced too. Even though the work people do is unrecognizable from the factory of the early twentieth century, thinking about managing people's performance hasn't moved at anywhere near the same pace. Management as a profession is ultra-conservative.

Outdated scientific management practices aren't helpful in the least. But more than that, they're holding businesses back from executing the nimbleness required. In other words, instead of helping—which is what performance management practices are supposed to do—they're hindering business. I explain how these management myths negatively impact on all the dimensions of agility. Several alternatives, based on a contemporary set of management beliefs, are advanced to promote agile performance. So a critical appraisal of the way we typically still manage performance promises to emancipate maneuverability, heighten flexibility, and increase speed.

Taylorism has, without doubt, a profound and ongoing influence on the traditional employment relationship. Performance management practices, with their foundation in scientific management—such as specialization and constructing work around jobs—have buttressed the conventional working relationship between management and labor. Changing well-entrenched performance management practices is ultimately futile without a fresh psychological contract between employer and employee. Unless a workplace—where new performance management practices are implemented—can cultivate a new working relationship or psychological contract, the new practices will be unsustainable. So the challenge is transforming organizational culture, based on a different set of expectations of the role of employee and manager.

Performance, learning, and culture go together. Speed, agility, and maneuverability are hamstrung in a workplace culture based on the traditional employment relationship characterized as "them and us." The demarcation of responsibilities in the old psychological contract is simple and clear-cut; that is, managers do the *thinking* and workers do the *doing*. Simplicity is one of the primary attractions of a "them and us" working relationship. Although straightforward, it's too basic to be effective in a climate of accelerated change and uncertainty. What's more, the conventional working arrangement is not conducive for agile behavior to flourish. The springboard for agile performance is a new, more collaborative, and far less delineated psychological contract. Knowing what that relationship should look like is the starting point for evaluating agile performance. Shifting this culture shouldn't be underestimated as a performance success factor.

Now, just a comment on how *Performance Management for Agile Organizations* is different from the plethora of books on organizational performance. I'm certainly not the first writer to be critical of such people management rituals as the performance review, hierarchical organizing structures, and the job description. I'm unlikely to be the last, either. Even if you've only read one or two books in the organization development field, you'd know that writers are critical of these, and other people management practices. But it seems that most of this critique has fallen on deaf ears or—more likely—the thinking behind managing performance is deeply entrenched, faulty, and hinders progress.

Notwithstanding the abundance of organizational performance advice, three things are novel about *Performance Management for Agile Organizations*. First, I describe my new model for evaluating organizational agility, which consists of seven dimensions. Second, I consider the eight management myths about performance that thwart speed and responsiveness. Discussing these psychological roadblocks makes what I hope is a compelling case for rethinking organizational performance. And third, I put forward a case and a framework for a culture based on a different kind of working relationship between employer and employee. Most performance management and organization development literature by-pass the psychological contract. It's often and incorrectly assumed that a new culture comes with applying new practices, rather than the reverse;

that is, different practices evolve from a new culture. So I take an uncommon approach to performance management.

If we continue to believe people (I am uncomfortable with the terms, *human resources* and *human capital*) are the competitive or adaptive advantage in business, we need to reflect on the assumptions we have about performance. How people in the work-setting interact and fuse with the bewildering assortment of systems, processes, and procedures, is the essence of performing at work. Scrutinizing how performance is managed is necessary, particularly now, when many of the time-honored systems are asphyxiating the capacity to work with agility.

I hope you enjoy my book and find it thought-provoking and practical.

Notes

1. Zheltoukhova, K. (2014). HR: Getting smart about agile working. CIPD research paper.
2. Economic Intelligence Unit (2009). *Organisational agility: How businesses can survive and thrive in turbulent times.* London: Economic Intelligence Unit.

Contents

Part I The Agile Enterprise   1

1 Profit Measures the Past—Agility Predicts the Future   3

2 The Characteristics of Agility   21

3 Seven Dimensions of Agile Performance   37

Part II Myths Blocking Agile Performance   57

4 Management Myth # 1—Job Specification Improves
   Performance   59

5 Management Myth # 2—Quality Systems and Processes
   Guarantee Good Outcomes   73

6 Management Myth # 3—The Job Description Helps
   the Employee Understand Their Organizational Role   89

7 Management Myth # 4—A Business is Best Organized
   around Functions   107

8 Management Myth # 5—A Satisfied Employee is a
   Productive Employee   125

9 Management Myth # 6—A Loyal Employee is an Asset
   to the Business   141

10 Management Myth # 7—A Technically Superior
   Workforce is a Pathway to a High-Performing Business   159

11 Management Myth # 8—Employees Can't Be Trusted
   with Sensitive Information   175

Part III   The Right Culture for Agile Performance   195

12 A New Psychological Contract for Managing Agile
   Performance   197

Index   219

About the Author

Tim Baker is a thought leader, international consultant, and successful author (www.winnersatwork.com.au). Tim was recently voted as one of *The 50 Most Talented Global Training & Development Leaders* by the World HRD Congress, which is awarded by a distinguished international panel of professionals "who are doing extraordinary work" in the field of HRD. Having completed his Doctoral degree in 2005 at QUT, Tim is a longstanding Member of QUT Council. He is the author of *The 8 Values of Highly Productive Companies: Creating Wealth from a New Employment Relationship* (Australian Academic Press), *The End of the Performance Review: A New Approach to Appraising Employee Performance* (Palgrave Macmillan), *Attracting and Retaining Talent: Becoming an Employer of Choice* (Palgrave Macmillan), *The New Influencing Toolkit: Capabilities for Communicating with Influence* (Palgrave Macmillan), co-author with Aubrey Warren of *Conversations at Work: Promoting a Culture of Conversation in the Changing Workplace* (Palgrave Macmillan), and *The End of the Job Description* (Palgrave Macmillan). Tim has conducted over 2430 seminars, workshops and keynote addresses to over 45,000 people in 11 countries across 21 industry groups and regularly writes for HR industry press. Tim can be contacted at tim@winnersatwork.com.au.

List of Figures

Fig. 3.1	Organizational agility model	45
Fig. 6.1	Performance management practices	92
Fig. 6.2	Model of work performance	101
Fig. 7.1	Functional model	110
Fig. 7.2	Matrix model	112
Fig. 7.3	Product model	113
Fig. 7.4	Customer-centric model	118
Fig. 11.1	Initiative paradox	182
Fig. 12.1	Psychological contract	201

List of Tables

Table 4.1   Skills matrix   69
Table 12.1 Traditional psychological contract framework   204
Table 12.2 New psychological contract framework   205

Part I

The Agile Enterprise

1

Profit Measures the Past—Agility Predicts the Future

Trevor Jones set up a meeting with Michelle Williams. They are plant managers in a large manufacturing business; both run the same operation at different locations. Trevor has been to Michelle's plant several times but hadn't really paid close attention to what they were doing there. He of course knew they made the same products, but it's difficult to rationalize the gap in performance between the two sites.

Michelle welcomed Trevor and asked him to join her in her plant's operations conference room. She also invited her leadership team, and they enthusiastically introduced themselves as Trevor got settled for the meeting.

"I hope you don't mind if I take a few notes," said Trevor. "I'm trying to understand why your plant is performing so much better than mine. You must set much higher goals for your workers to get the kind of results I've heard about."

"No, actually we haven't set goals this entire year," replied Michelle. "I decided to hold back on sharing the goals our boss gave us, and as the year

---

Even though profit and market share are fundamental measures of performance, the lenses used to examine, analyze and evaluate business success have become increasingly sophisticated. Yet many of our current people management practices are outdated and ineffective.

© The Author(s) 2017
T. Baker, *Performance Management for Agile Organizations*,
DOI 10.1007/978-3-319-40153-9_1

progressed we've slowly gained his trust to try this approach. Don't get me wrong; we still measure everything and track improvement trends, but we don't limit our thinking by setting goals."

"Limit your thinking; what do you mean?" asked Trevor.

"A little over a year ago, my leadership team and I decided to go through some training and team building together," explained Michelle. *"One of the activities in the class was a business simulation. The class was split into two teams and we were challenged to figure out how to improve the simulated business process in order to get the cost below a certain target. The team I was on calculated exactly how much product we needed to sell to hit the cost goal and then we designed our process to make that number. We ran the simulation and met all of the goals and thought that we had done very well. Then we found out that the other team had decided to ignore the goal and design their business process to reduce the cost as much as possible. They got very creative with the process design and came up with several innovative ideas for dramatic improvement. Their team ended up selling twice as much product and reduced their overall cost by over 50 per cent of what we had done. That was a real 'ah-ha' moment for all of us."*

"If there's a fear that goals could hamper your ability to dramatically improve, then why not set the objectives very high to try and motivate your employees?" inquired Trevor.

Mary's procurement manager spoke up. *"I worked for a company that once tried to use stretch goals, and it absolutely killed morale. In many cases, the stretch goal became THE goal, and your performance would get downgraded if you did not hit the stretch goal. And, if you did hit the stretch goal, then you clearly did not stretch far enough. So, either way, there was no way to win."*

"As we started discussing the impact goals have on the way we do things," Mary chimed in, *"we began to realize how our objectives were causing us to do really stupid things. It became clear that people were manipulating data to hit their targets instead of doing any real improvement."*[1]

Since the 1950s, there've been several schools of thought about how organization performance should be evaluated; each perspective building upon its predecessor. I'd like to map the progression of these well-established performance models here in the first chapter. Why do this? Well, I feel it's time to rethink organizational performance. Do we need to consider other ways of evaluating organizational performance? I think we do.

In particular, I want to introduce a new model of performance based on agility and its dimension (Chap. 3). What's more, there are many well accepted and entrenched people management practices that get in the way of responsiveness, speed, and innovation; all dimensions of agility. I'd like to shatter some of the myths these time-honored people management practices are based on.

But before going there, I think it helps to understand the evolution of how performance in organizations has been evaluated; what are the benefits and limitations of these approaches, and their impact. Although the need for agility is implicit in each model, I'm interested in building upon the current agility movement in the performance literature; it seems to be the next phase of performance evaluation. How quickly a business is responsive to an innumerable range of internal and external factors is now widely regarded as a source of competitive or adaptive advantage; this has been the case for at least the last two decades.[2] Despite this progress in the way we think about organizational performance, there are entrenched people management practices managers continue to cling to. These practices reduce—not increase—organizational agility.

But before considering these barriers, let's get back to basics. The ultimate business performance criterion is profit. By profit, I mean the marginal difference between business expenses or overheads and income or revenue. While profit will always be the focal point of any business enterprise, up until the mid-1950s it was regarded as the one and only means of measuring performance.

From the middle of the last century, organizational improvement scholars became deeply immersed in the best way for profit to be achieved and endured. Other models of performance flourished beyond the singular focus on profit. Various traits of organizational agility such as speed, maneuverability, flexibility, and responsiveness were linked to profitability and sustainability. The extent of agility was understood to be important for an enterprise to continually reach its outputs or objectives in a constantly changing marketplace. Agility for instance was considered increasingly vital in a climate of resource constraints, such as limited availability of capital and highly skilled employees. So unsurprisingly some of the characteristics of agility are at least inferred in the main models of organizational performance.

But performance has been measured in a variety of ways other than agility for the past 60 years or so. The first development from a solitary focus on profit—still prevalent today—was evaluating performing against a set of specific goals. With the goal-driven model, the organization is viewed as a closed system. The assumption supporting a closed system is that the business can control its destiny and is shielded from outside influences.

The significance of stakeholders and their bearing on performance became the next focus of analysis. There was a realization that stakeholders and their interests, particularly those beyond the boundaries of the organization, have a greater influence on business goals than was originally thought. The idea that an organization is an open system was born.

There was then a shift in emphasis from outputs to inputs and throughputs. The dominant question became: *How can organizations be more efficient and effective in achieving their goals and working with their stakeholders?* An orientation toward improving processes or throughputs was linked to high performance. The quality assurance (QA) movement originated from the process model.

A leading contemporary perspective is that the organization is a complex adaptive system; success is managing the myriad multi-faceted interrelationships that extend well beyond the physical gates of the business. The organization is viewed as a collection of dynamic and fluid systems and relationships requiring continual scrutiny and appraisal. Performance is highly dependent on the organization's capacity to adapt in complex environments. So the key to success is the capacity to be responsive and adaptive to the demands of a fluctuating and increasingly volatile marketplace.

Agility and its characteristics of speed, maneuverability, and flexibility in an open systems model is the driver of performance. Even though profit and market share are fundamental success factors, the lenses used to examine and analyze business performance are now very sophisticated.

Yet many of the people management practices still used are hopelessly outdated and ineffective.

> **Where the rubber meets the road ...**
>
> **Profit is the name of the game**
> I remember having an interesting conversation with a moderately successful business owner who was losing good employees and using primitive systems and processes to run his business. I recall him saying to me, "All I'm focused on is the bottom-line. Profit is the name of the game. All the other stuff is peripheral; it doesn't matter. My job is to maximize profit."
> At this point—as most consultants do—I asked him a clarifying question: "So your measure of organizational performance is the size of your profit margin, right?" "Yep," came the succinct reply.
> "What about the fact that you have told me you have high staff turnover, poor relations with your suppliers, and substandard systems and processes?" I challenged. "That's why you are here," he said with a smile; a smile I couldn't help returning!

Let's now consider each of these evolving schools of thought in more detail. I'll consider how each perspective built upon its predecessors, its strengths and limitations, and how it relates to the idea of agility.

The End Justifies the Means

The goal-driven model assesses performance on the basis of whether the business achieves its goals. From this perspective—which is still very popular in the corporate world—goals are commonly accepted as part of the business's culture, its design, and the way it's structured. In simple terms, the organization's purpose generally revolves around a set of specific goals.

The ultimate purpose of a business may be to generate a profit for its owners and shareholders. Using the goal model to achieve a profit, a business may set several goals, including a quantifiable return on equity, specific growth targets for revenue, increased market share, and a percentage reduction in costs associated with running the business. So organizational performance is evaluated against these goals.

Consider a different kind of organization—a not-for-profit enterprise. The purpose of this organization may be to fulfill a particular community need, such as catering for homeless people. Goals could be set to include the number of people using the service, the efficiency of its services in dealing with homeless people, the positive impact on the local community, and the ability to attract and retain government support through funding. Although a completely different set of goals, both entities—profit and not-for-profit—measure their success on the basis of whether their goals have been met.

The goal model is essentially an output focused approach to organizational performance. The analysis is on the end result, not necessarily the means of how it is—or can be—reached. The activities, behaviors, systems, processes, and procedures to achieve the goal are considered later, if at all. This is the main inadequacy of the model.

We've come to appreciate the significance of inputs for successful outputs. The original proponents of the goal-driven model of performance, however, focused attention on the relevance of specific, measurable goals.

Probably the most prominent goal model of performance—still very commonly used today, mainly in the sales focused enterprise—is Peter Drucker's "Management By Objectives" (MBO) approach. This goal-oriented model is still taught widely in reputable management schools and written about in organization development texts. It considers the primary criterion of performance—and the organization of work—to revolve around the accomplishment of the objectives necessary for success. Performance evaluation is based on whether the objectives have been met.

Although MBO was an early manifestation of the goal model, strategic planning and performance management are two contemporary people management practices based on this school of thought. These and other accepted and entrenched management practices reinforce the relevance of the goal model.

Like all performance models, the goal-driven approach is based on a set of beliefs. The basic assumption of the goal model is that people working in organizations are rational, deliberate, and goal-seeking. Another belief is that goals can be *specific, measurable, action-based, realistic,* and *time-limited* (S.M.A.R.T.). Organizational behavior, its policies and procedures, directives, priorities, and decisions, are shaped by S.M.A.R.T. goals.

Agile behavior in a goal-driven work environment is essentially expressed using the old Machiavellian quote: "the end justifies the means." In other words, whatever it takes to achieve the goal is acceptable practice as long as the goal is attained. In this context, agility is seen as an enabler for goal achievement.

Despite its clarity, straightforwardness, and popularity, the goal model has limitations. The most obvious drawback, as I alluded to earlier, is the model fails to adequately consider the inputs and throughputs needed to achieve the goal. Outputs are evaluated and inputs and throughputs run the risk of being by-passed, or at the very least, not evaluated with the same rigor.

Cutting corners, an absence of transparency, unfair or unethical action can prosper in the passionate pursuit of a goal. Processes, systems, and procedures are considered by whether they help or hinder a certain outcome. With this lack of scrutiny, poor behavior is permissible, can be ignored, or possibly encouraged if it enables the achievement of a certain goal.

Another limitation of the model is the possibility of employees being treated inequitably. Employees who are in a position to contribute directly to a goal, such as sales people chasing a sales goal for instance, can often receive favorable treatment. Preferential action in this case could mean better working conditions, generous financial incentives and perks, or more tolerance for substandard behavior.

On the contrary, employees who have an indirect role to perform in the achievement of business goals, such as those involved in the production of the product, can be undervalued, or devalued. Poorer working conditions, lesser pay, and a stricter code of behavior can result. Yet the contributions that these employees make are vital to business sales, albeit indirectly. As an illustration, producing the product faster with greater quality can translate ultimately to more sales. But the ancillary connection that these employees have to a sale's goal renders their work as possibly inconsequential. Not valuing the collective contribution to a successful outcome is a significant failing of the goal model.

We Are Not Operating in a Vacuum

The limitations of the goal model was the genesis of the systems model. This perspective is based on the belief that performance is best understood and accomplished by considering the organization as part of a bigger system. The ability to identify, understand, and control all the component parts of a system is the driver for superior performance in the systems model. Systems thinking means all factors within and outside the organization have potentially an important role to play in goal attainment.

The component parts of the system and their interaction with other parts, allow us to consider performance on a much larger scale than goal-setting. As an illustration, the spontaneous and successful acquisition of a scarce and valued resource, such as purchasing a quality investment or acquiring the business of a competitor, can have a major bearing on performance. Another illustration of how systems thinking is an entirely different approach to performance is organization development (OD). This prominent avenue of human resources development (HRD) is a field of research, theory, and practice dedicated to expanding the knowledge and effectiveness of people to accomplish more successful performance. OD has its roots in systems thinking.

The systems model however, doesn't replace the goal model; it builds upon it. What's more, systems thinking significantly improves an organization's goal-setting capability. Systems thinking has a dual focus. The goal model centers on outputs and the systems model focuses on the interactivities of the organization in a wider system to enable better outcomes. In simple terms, the goal method recognizes what gets done and the systems approach recognizes how it can get done. The systems approach therefore plugs a major deficiency of the goal approach.

What then are the distinguishing beliefs that guide and inform systems thinking? One assumption is that the system is made up of identifiable component parts or subsystems. Not only can the parts of a system be recognized, they can be evaluated in the context of overall performance. There's an assumption that the system's inputs, throughputs, and outputs are connected and that these subsystems are interdependent.

The systems model also works on the assumption that useful resources are available in the organization and should be utilized to improve performance. Management therefore has a responsibility to marshal administrative, technical, and human resources where they are needed within the system. So organizational performance is evaluated based on making judgments about how the system can work better.

Do we need more resources? Less? Can we be more flexible, agile, or quicker in the way we use our resources? These are the questions system thinkers ask. So the systems model, adopting a broader and more in-depth perspective of organizational performance than the goal model, focuses on balancing interdependencies and supporting performance throughout the system.

More than just assessing whether goals are achieved, the systems approach evaluates the activities within the organization on the basis of whether they lead to growth of the existing system. The advantage of observing the organization as a system is that managers can consider the performance of subsystems and whether they contribute or detract from organizational performance. Agility in this context is a preparedness to try new ways of optimizing subsystems.

On the other hand, one of the limitations of adopting a systems thinking approach to evaluate performance is the lure of becoming too myopic in one's perspective. Focusing on the efficiency or productivity of subsystems may constrict a manager's ability to adapt to subtle but significant fluctuations in the wider environment, including the marketplace. A blinkered view on subsystem optimization and integration can miss the bigger picture. Too much focus on systems can be as problematic as too much focus on outcomes. Both perspectives are important for organizational success.

> **Where the rubber meets the road ...**
>
> **A champion team will always beat a team of champions**
> An enterprise can be judged as high performing by assessing its superior subsystems, even though it might struggle to retain its competitive edge in the marketplace. Consider a popular sport's analogue: A team of stars—with outstanding individual skills—won't always defeat a superior team made up of players with average skill. Why? As the old cliché goes: "A champion team will always beat a team of champions." If the coach's attention is too focused on individual players and their skill development, the overall team performance may suffer. Improving subsystems doesn't always naturally translate into overall performance.

With the juggling act of balancing process and output, systems theory has evolved somewhat from its original thinking. Later versions of human systems models recognize the potential limitation of too much concentration on subsystems. What's more, there is an appreciation of the importance of engaging all the organization's stakeholders as part of the larger system. Systems thinking scholars have pointed out the significance of external forces beyond the direct control of management and their influence on organizational performance.[3] This comprehensive view is referred to as a complex adaptive system.

A sudden downturn in economic conditions, for example, may mean a business needs to rapidly move its concentration back to marketing established products. With this peripheral pressure, promoting a new, untested product line may not be a wise move. This sudden strategic change requires adaptivity. This form of agility will have implications for several subsystems, such as the marketing department, production, and suppliers. These unexpected situations aren't usually taken into consideration in the original systems model. These surprises require a rapid and constructive response, nevertheless. Being agile, responsive, and quick in these circumstances can make or break a business.

Paint by Numbers

A third school of thought about evaluating organizational performance is based on the process model. The process model builds on the foundations of both the goal and systems models. A strong emphasis is the internal processes an enterprise uses to achieve its goals. Goals are still used in process thinking to measure organizational performance. However, this perspective is more interested in goal optimization than goal achievement.

Goal optimization takes into account the various constraints and potential roadblocks facing the organization now and in the future; it recognizes market realities that limit or prevent goals from being accomplished. Once these factors have been identified, process thinking considers ways to adapt employee behavior to meet these circumstances. Briefly, the process model shifts the weight from the organization as a whole to the behavior of individuals.

The belief supporting this model is that if employees have buy-in to the goals of the business, they'll probably support and contribute to the goals enthusiastically. Aligning the needs of the individual with the interests of the organization is the ultimate aim of the process model. The use of the "balanced score card" is a popular performance management practice of the process model in action. The balanced score card is a performance measurement system that provides a comprehensive view of progress toward achieving strategic goals. Improvement is measured in both financial and nonfinancial terms. The process method focuses attention on key performance indicators (KPIs) within the organization to measure performance.

Goals or outcomes are still relevant, as I mentioned. And in terms of systems thinking, subsystems such as customers, employees, and internal operations are taken into consideration in process development. With improvement in mind, balancing processing speed and quality is paramount. Quality assurance is a spin-off of process modelling.

The well-documented example of the process model of business performance in action is the McDonald's franchising system. In this system, processes are thought through, documented, and regimented. The process model shares similar beliefs of proponents of the systems model; that is, internal processes and organizational outcomes are causal to end results. If you follow the system, you'll get a predictable result or outcome. It can be described as a "paint by numbers" approach.

Boundaries can be identified within the system and resources can be adjusted to improve performance. Setting goals, identifying and removing—or at least minimizing— roadblocks, and developing superior processes is the essence of process thinking. There is an underlying belief that internal processes are crucial for success and inextricably linked to performance.

On the downside, this approach doesn't routinely take into account external factors like economic downturns, legislative changes, or socioeconomic trends. The agility of the organization to capitalize on or minimize these instabilities, can be hamstrung with the process model. Peripheral awareness—more prevalent in other performance models—is imperative; there is little doubt the outlying setting is a major factor in the success or otherwise of any enterprise.

Being too fixated on internal processes will inevitably distract the business from subtle outside influences and pressures. At best, process thinking can result in sluggishness when a response is necessary. And at worst, process fixation can wipe out a business. Despite its limitations, superior processes unquestionably build performance capacity and improve the quality of outcomes.

The Political Organization

The stakeholder model has evolved with an appreciation that stakeholders in the orbit of an organization have diverse perspectives. These various stakeholder viewpoints need to be taken into account; they inevitably have an impact on organizational performance. Viewing organizational performance through the eyes of the stakeholder begins with understanding their motives and adapting to accommodate their viewpoint. I define key stakeholders as any individual or group that has a vested interest in the success or failure of a particular organization.

For example, stakeholders may include employees, pressure groups, unions, advisors and consultants, agents, franchisees, governing bodies, and investors. Stakeholders can have a direct or indirect relationship with an organization. To illustrate, employees, agents, franchisees, and investors all derive a direct benefit from a high-performing organization; or are negatively affected by poor performance. Indirect stakeholders may include pressure groups, such as unions and employer groups, and regulators who impose control and regulations on the organization. From an individual stakeholder's perspective, a high performance organization is one that is able to satisfy their particular needs; or at least lessen the negative demands on them. This performance perspective implies that organizations are a political entity; one that bargains with and attempts to satisfy the complex array of stakeholders it has to deal with.

This outlook is a departure from the goal, systems, and process models. The stakeholder model identifies its key stakeholders, understands their drivers, and does what it can to gain leverage from these networks. An organization evaluating its performance against the stakeholder model, ties success to the multitude of stakeholders and constituencies it deals with.

Many government agencies and instrumentalities fall into this category. So the stakeholder model measures organizational performance through its role in the political arena; where stakeholders with varying degrees of power vie for control over resources. These resources can be human, technical, or administrative.

To complicate matters, each stakeholder group has a unique perspective and a distinctive set of needs to be fulfilled. The central beliefs supporting the stakeholder model are based on survival, sustainability, and viability. Key performance drivers therefore center on maintaining the organization's position and retaining its legitimacy in the political system it operates in.

The vested interests of stakeholders are the central focal point in the model. The strength of this performance perspective is its consciousness of the multiple stakeholders the organization engages with; and the realization that addressing their needs is key to its success. Questions like: *Who are our key stakeholder groups? What are their primary motivations and interests? How can they be satisfied?* are dominant in stakeholder thinking. Addressing these innumerable interests and driving forces is the bottom-line of success.

One of the apparent limitations of this approach is the unavoidable bias an organization will display toward one or more stakeholder groups. Apart from power over the organization, no rational basis for favoring one stakeholder group over another is evident. It is the stakeholder's potential influence and nothing else that counts; attention and resources are driven by power. Though pragmatic, this favoritism means other stakeholders—who don't receive the same attention and resources—can be estranged. This can lead to unintentional negative consequences for the organization.

The agility needed here is the organization's capacity to respond swiftly and decisively to powerful stakeholder interests. Power-bases can quickly and dramatically shift in a dynamic environment, depending on the circumstances. High-performing organizations are able to read and respond to the rise and fall of stakeholder influence. The agile organization can change its focus and priorities at the right time and place.

Goals are still relevant in satisfying the demands of stakeholders; the stakeholder model adopts a systems thinking approach; and correct processes are important. So the stakeholder model builds on the attributes of the other three models. But it goes a step further. It considers performance in the context of the political realities of dealing with an array of stakeholder interests.

One Size Doesn't Fit All

The competing values model acknowledges that there are multiple and conflicting principles at play in organizational performance. "One size doesn't fit all," is the familiar saying that sums up this school of thought. The competing values approach appreciates that high-performing organizations have a variety of values that are often in conflict with one another. So performance is largely about how these clashes are managed.

These contradictory interests can be mapped according to the competing values model. As a useful frame-of-reference, competing value-sets can be typically distilled into three core dichotomies:

- internal versus external environment;
- flexibility versus control; and
- process versus outcome.

As you can see, these value-sets represent polar opposites and therefore clash with one another. There are other value clashes too. For example, values that focus on people and values that focus on tasks are contrasting. Or the idea of displaying initiative versus maintaining compliance is a diametrically opposite set of values. These contending values are a reality of organizational life. Apart from mapping these conflicting values, the competing values model attempts to resolve these apparent contradictions.

Let's consider this in more detail. If performance is assessed on the values of compliance and regulation—familiar in most government agencies—these values are at odds with values espousing creative problem-solving. Or the values of control and hierarchy in a military or paramilitary organization are in conflict with the values of enterprise and flexibility. A business that values expansion and growth clashes with the values of consolidating and refining internal processes, procedures, and systems. These dilemmas are present in every enterprise.

To illustrate the point, 60 per cent of HR managers in the public sector in the UK categorized their organization as having values aligned with an internal focus as distinct from an external focus, and a greater degree of control than flexibility.[4] The key question for managers then, when evaluating their organization's performance using this model is: *How can conflicting value-sets coexist and be valid drivers of behavior?*

While the notion of embracing competing values seems odd, it doesn't mean they can't concur within the same organization. What's more, it's desirable to nurture polar opposite value-sets for high performance. An organization for instance, can value stability and be steady on the one hand, and value flexibility and be malleable on the other. Despite inherent contradictions in organizational structures and systems that lead to either stability or flexibility, it is widely acknowledged that both competencies are vital for success. Performance is evaluated on the basis of an enterprise's successfully sponsoring polar opposite values. But how?

Organizations can accommodate both sets of values through structural methods of differentiation. This is called "organizational ambidexterity,"[5] defined as a

> work flow model that encourages both exploration and exploitation by building separate organizational units tasked with the dissimilar goals associated with these activities, or by creating temporal separation in the sequencing of organizational activities.[6]

Performance is improved by using systems and processes that permit the contrasting values of alignment and adaptability to be expressed simultaneously.

Agility in this context means two things: first, the rapid adjustment between these competing values. Making speedy and correct adjustments between alignment and adaptability is based on the situation. For example, if the situation is a health and safety matter, alignment activities such as following correct procedures wins out. But exploiting new market opportunities—such as intelligence gathering and market research—requires behavior that's adaptable. So performing is defined as the ability to move swiftly and systematically between two competing sets of values, such as alignment and adaptability, depending upon the situation and circumstances. The second aspect of agility using the competing values model is the speedy completion of the tasks and activities of each response.

To perform with organizational ambidexterity, you need well trained employees, apart from good systems and processes. Managing competing values is the basis for modern "complexity theory,"[7] as it applies to the agile enterprise. The competing values model can be useful for business improvement and development in a marketplace demanding a diverse range of organizational responses.

But a limitation of this school of thought is that evaluating performance is not clear-cut. For instance, success is harder to measure than in the goal model, with its clear KPIs. It's a challenge, in other words, to answer the following question with clarity: *How well is the organization performing in accommodating sets of competing values?*

In conclusion, I've briefly explained the five trends in evaluating organizational performance since the mid-twentieth century. The original success measure was profit alone. Each successive model builds on its predecessors, offering a more complete analysis of enterprise performance. They each have their benefits and weaknesses, nevertheless. We're presently in the midst of a sixth phase, emphasizing agility as the key driver of performance; it's well documented that agility is critical to organizational performance.[8] Contributing to the agility performance movement, I offer a model for evaluating organizational agility in Chap. 3.

Before I explain the model, I'd like to define the characteristics of the agile enterprise in the next chapter.

The Top 10 Key Points …

1. The goal model assesses performance on the basis of whether or not the business has achieved its goals.
2. The goal model fails to adequately consider the inputs and throughputs needed to achieve the goal.

3. The systems model is based on the belief that performance is best understood and accomplished by considering the organization as part of a bigger system. The component parts of the system, and their interaction between each other, consider performance on a much larger scale.
4. One of the possible limitations of adopting a systems thinking approach to performance evaluation is the lure of becoming too myopic in one's perspective.
5. The process model emphasizes the internal processes an enterprise uses to achieve its goals.
6. One of the downsides of the process model is that it doesn't routinely take into account external factors like economic downturns, legislative changes, or socio-economic trends.
7. The stakeholder model has developed from an acceptance that stakeholders in the organizational orbit inevitably have different perspectives and should to be taken into account when evaluating organizational performance.
8. One of the apparent limitations of the stakeholder model is the unavoidable bias toward one or more stakeholder groups at the expense of others.
9. The competing values model acknowledges that there are multiple and conflicting values relevant to organizational success.
10. The limitation of the competing values model is it doesn't offer definitive measures of performance, such as those in the goal model.

Notes

1. Dyer, J. (2013). Does management by objectives stifle excellence? http://www.industryweek.com/lean-six-sigma/does-management-objectives-stifle-excellence?page=3
2. Harraf, A., Wanasika, I., Tate, K., & Talbott, K. (2015). Organizational agility. *The Journal of Applied Business Research*, 31 (2).
3. Martz, W. (2013). Evaluating organizational performance: Rational, natural, and open systems models. *American Journal of Evaluation*, 34 (3), 385–401.

4. Economic Intelligence Unit (2009). *Organisational agility: How businesses can survive and thrive in turbulent times.* London: Economic Intelligence Unit.
5. Patel, P.C., Messersmith, J.G., & Lepak, D.P. (2013). Walking the tightrope: An assessment of the relationship between high-performance work systems and organizational ambidexterity. *Academy of Management Journal*, 56 (5), 1420–1442.
6. Ibid.
7. Martz, W. (2013). Evaluating organizational performance: Rational, natural, and open systems models. *American Journal of Evaluation*, 34 (3), 385–401.
8. Harraf, A., Wanasika, I., Tate. K., & Talbott, K. (2015). Organizational agility. *The Journal of Applied Business Research*, 31 (2).

2

The Characteristics of Agility

Customers want constant improvement in the products they purchase. Many retailers strive for outstanding service and attractive store designs, but few go to Apple's lengths in incessantly improving every detail.

Take store design, for example. According to Brian Dyches, president of industry group, Retail Design Institute, "most retailers take a prototype and roll it out." Apple by contrast "constantly evolves its stores' look and feel." Apple stores, for example, have removed that ubiquitous, but irritating feature of retail stores—the cash register. Sales people complete their transactions on mobile devices.

Instead of starting with what Apple has to sell, the sales staff start from where the customer is, and what the customer's problem might be. Apple operationalizes its "steps of service" in the simple acronym APPLE:

Approach customers with a personalized warm welcome;
Probe politely to understand all the customer's needs;

A successful business of the twentieth century was characterized as stable, predictable, and conforming. The polar opposite is true now. A high-performing business of the twenty-first century is constantly able to remain in a state of instability, changeability, and non-conformity.

Present a solution for the customer to take home today;
Listen for and resolve any issues or concerns; and
End with a fond farewell and an invitation to return.[1]

Now that we've considered the evolving methods of evaluating organizational performance, in this chapter, I want to describe the standout characteristics of the agile enterprise. Agility is doubtlessly the current criteria for performance success. So it's essential to understand the characteristics of an agile enterprise in action. We'll then turn our attention to the seven dimensions of agility in Chap. 3. But without a clear definition of its conditions, the agile enterprise is a vague idea, open to all sorts of interpretations and misunderstandings.

Chapter 3—the final chapter in Part I—identifies the dimensions used to evaluate agile performance. While there are cross-overs between the characteristics of the agility and how it should be evaluated, there's a fundamental difference between the two concepts. So in this chapter, I define the characteristics of agility before exploring the ways it can be evaluated, in the next chapter.

Being agile is no longer an option for a business, if it wants to remain successful. The relentless and rapidly transforming marketplace means a business must have the capability to be maneuverable and responsive to retain and grow their market share. Surviving in a tumultuous economy is one test, but staying one step ahead of the competition is another. But these two challenges have one common thread: the need for agile performance. To use a metaphor: Surfing the fast and unpredictable waves of a volatile ocean involves courage, resourcefulness, adaptability, responsiveness, and speed. Surviving and thriving—as I pointed out in Chap. 1—is about ambidexterity; that is, the business must value both consolidation and stability and apply them in the right places and at the right time.

Although seemingly strange bed fellows, both sets of values must coexist in a seamless and harmonious way under the same roof. While being skilled at using both hands adeptly, performance is more dependent than ever on agile thinking and behavior. What's more, reaching and sustaining high performance is reliant on exercising several dimensions of agility. Agility isn't a technique, a fad, or a process; it's not so much what organizations do, it's more how its members think about what they do.

Agility has to permeate the culture of a business, including its teams and individuals, and the way business gets done.

A successful business of the twentieth century was characterized as stable, predictable, and conforming. The polar opposite is true now. A high-performing business of the twenty-first century is constantly able to remain in a state of instability, changeability, and non-conformity. In the current marketplace, everything has to be accomplished faster, with greater flexibility, almost instantaneously. So it is unsurprising that there is a burgeoning interest in agile performance in business.

The globalization of the marketplace has lessened or removed boundaries between countries, markets, technology, stakeholders, and customers. The world is becoming more and more interconnected, smaller—yet more complex. Everything done in an enterprise can be outsourced. Partnerships and alliances in the business world are forming that were considered unthinkable a decade ago. Having a competitive edge is a temporary state. Global rivalry for market share is intensifying. Customers are more demanding; they've got more choices and a bewildering array of options at the click of a button. Above all, customers want low prices, high quality, and warp speed delivery. It's a tough, uncompromising environment to do business in.

Beyond these competitive pressures, the speed of technological advancement and the uncertainty this raises, means managers need a crystal ball instead of a strategic plan. This explosion in technological innovation appears never ending. The knowledge explosions are getting louder, bigger, and more impactful. Everything is travelling at the speed of light. Ready and immediate access to an abundance of information is problematic, particularly when quick decisions have to be made. Business leaders have to make split-second decisions about what data is relevant—and what isn't—while being bombarded with information and knowledge from left, right, and center. Turbulence is the norm and responsiveness the challenge.

Disruption is everywhere, every day. Without accurate assessment of trends, business leaders can go from penthouse to the s**thouse in a matter of months. Consider *Borders*, the once profitable book-selling chain. By the mid-1990s, *Amazon* launched as an online book retailer and Borders made a serious strategic blunder. Instead of following *Barnes &*

Noble in moving online, Borders went international, building a substantial chain in the United Kingdom and opening stores as far away from the United States as Singapore. This global expansion seems to have blurred the focus of Borders' business in the USA. Ultimately, the international strategy failed. Borders also was slower than it should have been in adopting new techniques for marketing. Big mistake in hindsight; and costly too![2] Being responsive and quick to change direction could've meant a dramatically different outcome for Borders.

Amanda Setili, author of *The Agility Advantage*, puts a convincing case that companies have no option: they must learn to be more nimble and agile. In her book, she cites the cautionary tale of *Microsoft*:

> While the company had enviable profit performance under former CEO Steve Ballmer, it focused too much on protecting their historically strong products, Windows and Office. They failed to make the changes necessary to succeed in the smartphone and tablet markets, and as a result, their share of internet-connected devices declined from 90 percent in 2009 to only about 20 percent today.[3]

The two cases of Borders and Microsoft illustrate the problems that can occur with well-established firms suffering from a lack of agility thinking.

The landscape I've painted seems bleak. It's only bleak if we think about resolving the challenges I just described with the same thought and tools. But it's a new landscape; a canvas with exciting prospects that requires an artist with fresh ideas and a new set of paint brushes.

> **Where the rubber meets the road ...**
>
> **Capability without interoperability**
> As Commanding General of the Joint Special Operations Command, General Stanley McChrystal faced this problem I'm about to describe in real time. Although he commanded the most effective military machine ever designed, and could win any battle, he couldn't predict where those battles would be. In his new book, *Team of Teams*,[4] he describes how he reengineered his organization to not merely execute, but to continuously adapt. In Iraq in 2004, General McChrystal was facing his own disruptive threat. His forces completely outclassed the enemy. Yet no matter how many they killed or how many battles they won, new terrorists kept popping up elsewhere.

(continued)

McChrystal didn't think the problem was one of capability, but "interoperability." His forces would kill or capture Al Qaeda operatives and collect valuable intelligence, such as documents and hard drives. Yet it often took weeks for the prisoners to be questioned and the data to be analyzed. By that time, the information was often no longer relevant or actionable.

Another challenge was with how information flowed. Intelligence analysts were adept at turning raw data into actionable insights, but following protocol, they passed that information up the chain-of-command, where it was passed on to military planners, who would then develop strategies for the troops on the ground. This created further lags.

All in all, McChrystal's military machine was working as it was designed—each subunit was performing to the highest standards—but the design itself was not suited to the task. As McChrystal has said, "it takes a network to defeat a network."

What the General saw was that the problem wasn't how his forces did their jobs, but *how they saw their jobs*. Commandos strived to conduct raids with deadly precision, reconnaissance teams were focused on keeping an eye on the enemy, intelligence analysts wanted to develop insights about the enemy. Yet the shared mission—defeating Al Qaeda—was being lost.

So McCrystal set out to create a "shared consciousness," by creating connections between teams. He redesigned the command post to encourage interaction, embedded intelligence analysts with commandos and *vice versa*, and held daily status calls that included all of the diverse stakeholders. That allowed people to look beyond their own jobs and "see the system."

It was that shared sense of purpose that enabled him to empower his forces on the ground. But as the General stresses, the sequence is important. As he writes, "an organization should empower its people, but only *after* it has done the heavy lifting of creating shared consciousness." That's how he transformed his command into a "team of teams" and prevailed.

While all of this stress on interoperability reduced the efficiency of his teams somewhat, the overall productivity of the organization improved by a *factor of 19*. In an age of disruption, the only viable strategy is to adapt. Leaders today can no longer afford to think in conventional terms of efficiency, but must shape networks in the context of a shared mission.

Agility enables nimble adaption and quick responses in the landscape I've just described; the one you and I are part of. So agility is tied to organizational success, particularly commercial success. Speed and responsiveness, the two constant components of agility, are drivers of performance. Coping with the environment I've just described—and competing successfully with other companies—is predominantly about speed and responsiveness. Like lots of things in life, knowing this is the easy part; executing it is the tough part.

So what are the characteristics of the agile enterprise?

Professor Abe Harraf and his colleagues recently identified a set of characteristics of an agile organization. In their article, *Organizational Agility*, the authors identify 15 features that describe the agile enterprise.[5] Harraf et al.'s framework was developed after a comprehensive analysis of the research on agility. I'll briefly cover these characteristics here.

Just to be clear: The following 15 characteristics are key ingredients for promoting agile behavior in an organizational context. My model, instead, identifies how an organization should evaluate their performance at being agile.

I should also make the point that there is a considerable difference in ideas of the determinants of agility in the burgeoning books on the subject. Nevertheless, there is general agreement on the organizational characteristics of agility.

Characteristic # 1—The Innovation Mindset

Without creating a culture conducive for innovation, it's unlikely that an enterprise will grow and develop. A culture of innovation is one that's constantly evaluating everything: its systems, structures, procedures, teams, goals, capabilities, culture, and so on. Nothing is off limits for constructive criticism. The innovation mindset is more than an openness to change; it's an attitude of striving for new and better ways of performing everything. There are several barriers—based on management myths—to creating this kind of culture; I cover these in Part II.

Characteristic # 2—Seeking Out Improvement Opportunities

Closely aligned with the innovation mindset, is being continually on the lookout for improvement opportunities. An innovation culture is characterized by being on the lookout for ways and means of improving the current policies, procedures, systems, and practices in the business. Continuous improvement is being both proactive and reactive. It's not only about being alert to opportunities for improvement and responding to these situations. Continuous improvement is also actively seeking out enhancement opportunities, even when they're not so obvious. And once recognized, it's also concerned with doing something to change and improve the system, situation, or circumstance. This characteristic entails an attitude of relentlessly looking for new opportunities for development, being open and constructively critical of the way things are done, and being creative and willing to consider out-of-the-box solutions. Again, some well-known people management practices—such as specialization—interfere with this type of thinking.

Characteristic # 3—Empowerment and Enablement

Empowerment is doubtlessly the most overused word in the management lexicon. Briefly, empowerment is

> a management practice of sharing information, rewards, and power with employees so that they can take initiative and make decisions to solve problems and improve service and performance.[6]

Enablement means "to provide (someone) with adequate power, means, opportunity, or authority (to do something)."[7] So together, empowerment and enablement are equipping people with the capacity to act. An employee's capacity to act depends largely on the type of working relationship they have with their immediate boss. Specifically, it involves the authority the employees have been given by their manager to make decisions, and the amount of autonomy and freedom they have to action these decisions.

An agile enterprise is an organization with power spread evenly throughout, regardless of rank and status. To enable real empowerment, an organization's decision-making processes must be decentralized, rather than centralized. Traditional notions of hierarchical power and 'seniority' stifle empowerment and enablement.

Characteristic # 4—Decentralization of Power

Responsiveness to the mad marketplace I described earlier, is accomplished by dispersing power widely and deeply. Business is more agile when the employee at the "coal face" has the authority to make decisions without always checking with their boss. When this devolution of power is present, the quantity and quality of proactive behavior is more often and more apt. It is, however, well documented that centralized power has its place, especially in a big crisis. In these emergency situations, top management needs to "cut through" and make quick decisions, particularly when the crisis is widespread and high risk.

The agile enterprise exercises power with nimbleness—fluctuating between centralization and decentralization—depending upon the circumstances. It appears to be contradictory, but rudimentary decentralized decision-making, rather than centralization, enhances an organization's overall agility. Traditional ideas about centralized power and control often prevent devolved decision-making beyond managerial ranks.

Characteristic # 5—A Tolerance for Ambiguity

Working with uncertainty is now the norm. With an escalation of volatility and unpredictability, there's no longer the *one* orthodox method of responding to marketplace challenges. The agile enterprise flourishes in the face of ambiguity. A tolerance for ambiguity is the obligatory attitude for success. Established people management practices that stress clarity and certainty—such as the job description—are obsolete (Chap. 6). Being able to adapt is the new standard.

Tolerance for ambiguity is a different attribute to market responsiveness, although they work in tandem. While tolerance for ambiguity is the acceptance of the need to be adaptable, market responsiveness is the capacity to act in the face of ambiguity.

Characteristic # 6—Vision and Focus

The vision for an enterprise should have two primary purposes: to inspire employees and retain focus. A vision must be inspirational to some degree. *To provide the very best customer service* is hardly likely to get employees out of bed excited to come to work in the morning! The challenge of the vision should be "out of reach, but not unreachable"; in other words, it needs to test organizational members. A vision needs to inform; it responds to the question: *Where are we heading?* You've no doubt seen vision statements extend to one or two pages in length. A powerful vision can be captured in one simple sentence. The best vision statements are straightforward; they aren't complicated. And finally, the vision should be a call-to-action; it should instigate a certain type of activity. Everything that happens (or doesn't happen) in an enterprise ought to move the business closer—directly or indirectly—toward realizing the vision.[8] Agility can then be expressed and justified on the basis of a clear focus and destination.

Characteristic # 7—Commitment to the Strategic Direction

The direction of an enterprise is guided by the vision. I define *strategic direction* in this context as the desire and commitment to reach the optimum state: the vision. Many performance management practices derail this desire and commitment. Functional-based work structures, for example, can create unnecessary boundaries between departments that obscure the vision (Chap. 7). The vision statement by itself doesn't promote agile behavior. It's the way the vision is communicated and the organizational culture and practices that make the difference between agility and clumsiness.

Strategic direction is the capacity to produce a laser sharp focus on the vision. Clarity of direction and unwavering focus provide a sense of confidence business needs to be successful. With the right climate and tools, it encourages agility too. As long as the vision is inspirational, challenging, clear, and straightforward, it opens up a scope of possibilities of how the business can arrive at the desired destination. Agility prospers with a laser beam focus.

Characteristic # 8—Leading the Way

Leadership is crucial for keeping a company's concentration on the strategic direction. The CEO and the senior team are the custodians of the strategic direction. Their actions and inactions set the tone for what is acceptable and unacceptable practice. Agile enterprises make most of their decisions with speed and conviction. It's a management myth that decentralized decision-making structures sacrifice speed. In reality, a frontline employee, led the right way, tends to make quick and accurate decisions. Leadership commitment to decentralized decision-making gives the frontliner more confidence to "back themselves" and be decisive. Ironically, in organizations with a devolution of power, greater numbers of decisions are made. What's more, accuracy improves and responsiveness increases. Good leadership leads to timeliness, speed, and effective execution. Also, people actively engaged in the decision-making process are generally supportive and less resistant to the outcomes of those decisions. Put simply, if employees *own* the decisions, they feel accountable for the outcomes.

Characteristic # 9—Managing Change

I define change management in this instance as managing the enterprise's transition to its vision; its desired future state. Change and agility are inseparable. People—even though they don't necessarily feel comfortable with it—understand that change is inevitable, and even desirable. Managing any change successfully has three essential phases. First, there is a perceived need for change. Without an apparent need for change, there's no pressure to deviate from the *status quo*; the proposal gets put in the "too hard basket." Second, there is the need to execute the change efficiently and effectively. Implementing change is about accomplishing actionable outcomes. And third, the change needs to be tested. Once a change is realized, the results require evaluation. *What lessons have been learnt? Has the change been successful? How could it have been done better?* are some constructive questions that should be addressed. Most change management initiatives fail because at least one of these three phases have been poorly thought through and executed. But agile enterprises—always in a state of flux and change—carry these three phases out better than most.

Characteristic # 10—Effective Communication

The way an organization communicates (or doesn't communicate) internally to its members and externally to its stakeholders and customers will determine its capacity to be agile. Effective communication is necessary for managing change and everything else, for that matter.

But communication is more complicated with change. The decision about when to exercise centralized and decentralized decision-making isn't always straightforward. Communicating a proposed course-of-action and gathering feedback across the organization during a busy time, although important, is time consuming. We're all familiar with leaders who by-pass this communication imperative in the interests of "saving time." The management myth that *employees can't be trusted with sensitive information* (Chap. 11), reinforces or justifies this lack of engagement with employees. But without a free flowing communication channel, employees can equate proactive behavior with career diminution.

Characteristic # 11—Building Teams

But decentralized decision-making and open communication are improved with cross-functional project teams (Chap. 7). These project teams are formed to take more responsibility away from functional areas, break down silos, and execute change across the organization. How effective these teams are depend on many factors, including their composition and role.

Cross-functional project teams go against the grain of the traditional functional organizing structure. In other words, cross-functional teams are counter to the common siloed structure that's been in existence for over 100 years. Even so, the organization-wide collaboration derived from cross-functional teamwork is characteristic of the agile enterprise; teamwork is paramount to its success.

Characteristic # 12—Market Responsiveness

Business can't exist without a market. Being able to analyze and respond to the needs of the market landscape I described earlier in the chapter is a characteristic of the agile enterprise. Analysis and responsiveness are inextricably linked. Without thorough and ongoing analysis, the firm's responsiveness diminishes. Having the tools to analyze the company's positioning and standing in their industry sector and the marketplace they service enables timely adjustments to be made.

While the other 14 characteristics are internally focused, this characteristic of the agility enterprise emphasizes the external environment the business operates in. Agility can't be completely confined to the internal operations of a business; as proponents of the systems and stakeholder models of performance would rightly point out. Being agile requires keeping a close eye on competition and the external environmental setting.

Characteristic # 13—Maximizing Efficiency and Effectiveness

Apart from understanding and responding to the wider milieu, managing operations within the business involves an ongoing commitment to maximizing efficiency and effectiveness. Efficiency and effectiveness are both essential, but different, interventions.

Efficiency refers to the capacity to complete operations with minimum effort, resources, and time, without forgoing quality. For example, processing customer orders in a business requires efficiency. *Effectiveness* involves timing and priority: the right action, at the right time, and in the right way. Effectiveness, for example, would involve me deciding what the best use of my time would be, and how I might go about executing the activity (or inactivity!) chosen for maximum impact. Both are characteristic of the agile enterprise.

Maximizing efficiency and effectiveness in operational matters is only possible when an employee is encouraged and enabled to consider and seek out faster, better ways of doing their work tasks and activities. This attitude must extend to the supply chain too. Although, this line of thinking runs counter to the philosophy and systems of QA; another established people management practice (Chap. 5).

Characteristic # 14—Structural Fluidity

Organizational structure has a big bearing on a company's ability to be flexible, responsive, and maneuverable. Structure covers the full gambit of how a business initiates, performs, and finishes its work. The structure of an organization is the guiding framework that drives performance. Structure specifically shapes the links between people and operations and communication channels. It affects the vision, enables or hinders flexibility and agility, and influences responsiveness. Rigid organizing structures—without structural fluidity—choke agile thinking and behavior (Chap. 7).

The agile enterprise tends to be flat, boundary-less, customer-focused, and structured around teams, not functions. These features support structural fluidity.

Characteristic # 15—Development of a Learning Organization

According to Abe Harraf and his colleagues, the final characteristic in their agility framework—development of a learning organization—is the culmination of the other characteristics. A *learning organization*, first conceptualized by Peter Senge over 25 years ago, inspires its members to be in a continual state of growth and learning. Perpetual development of the workforce thwarts organizational stagnation and is supposed to turbo charge performance.

Agility and learning are inseparable—a point I expand upon in the next chapter. The learning organization is an agile organization and *vice versa*. Learning and continuous human capacity improvement fuels the attributes of openness and responsiveness. Every aspect of the work-setting is potentially an opportunity to learn from and improve upon.

These 15 characteristics of organizational agility aren't new. But together they provide a framework for defining the agile enterprise. The application of these characteristics varies from organization to organization. However, together they provide an understanding of what is necessary to be agile. What's more, they provide managers with a useful roadmap.

In the next chapter—the final chapter in Part I—I introduce my Organizational Agility model. The seven dimensions of agility are the basis for evaluating organizational performance. As I mentioned at the beginning of this chapter, there is some overlap between the 15 characteristics discussed here and the seven dimensions of agility covered in the next chapter. But to be clear, the model I'm about to describe is a new model for evaluating organizational performance, based on seven dimensions. I hope it adds some value to the discussion we've had in Chap. 1 on the evolution of thought around assessing organizational performance.

The Top 10 Key Points ...

1. Without creating a culture of innovation, it's unlikely that an organization will be able to exercise any agility. Aligned with the culture of innovation, is the notion of being continually on the lookout for opportunities for improvement.
2. An agile enterprise is organized on a decentralized model of power to make decisions across and down the organization, regardless of rank and status. Responsiveness to the frenetic marketplace is accomplished from decentralizing power structures.
3. Agile enterprises thrive in the face of ambiguity. Similar to innovation, a tolerance for ambiguity is the obligatory mindset needed.
4. The vision equips the organization with the scaffolding for the countless decisions that need to be made and the provision of a guide for suitable organizational behavior. Agility can then be expressed in myriad ways on the journey to that destination. Leadership is a critically important factor in keeping a company's concentration on the strategic direction.

5. Successfully managing change and agility are inextricably linked.
6. The way an organization communicates (or doesn't communicate) internally to employees and externally to stakeholders and customers will determine, to a large extent, its scope for agility.
7. Decentralized decision-making and communication can be promoted with the formation of cross-functional project teams.
8. Having the tools to analyze the company's position and standing in their industry and the marketplace enables timely adjustments to be made. Apart from understanding and responsiveness to the wider milieu, managing operations within the business involves maximizing efficiency and effectiveness.
9. Organizational structure has a big bearing on a company's ability to be flexible, responsive, and maneuverable.
10. Learning and continuous improvement fuels the attributes of openness and responsiveness.

Notes

1. Denning, S. (2011). Apple's retail success is more than magic. http://www.forbes.com/sites/stevedenning/2011/06/17/apples-retail-stores-more-than-magic/
2. Osnos, P. (2011). What went wrong at Borders. http://www.theatlantic.com/business/archive/2011/01/what-went-wrong-at-borders/69310/
3. Setili, A. (2014). *The agility advantage: How to identify and act on opportunities in a fast-changing world.* Jossey-Bass.
4. McChrystal, S., Collins, T., Silverman, D., & Fussell, C. (2015). *Team of teams: New rules of engagement for a complex world.* Penguin.
5. Harraf, A., Wanasika, I., Tate, K., & Talbott, K. (2015). Organizational agility. *The Journal of Applied Business Research*, 31 (2).
6. http://www.businessdictionary.com/definition/empowerment.html#ixzz3nO41tvUj
7. http://dictionary.reverso.net/english-definition/enablement
8. Baker, T. (2015). *The end of the job description: Shifting from a job-focus to a performance-focus.* London: Palgrave Macmillan.

3

Seven Dimensions of Agile Performance

The Australasian Legal Practice Management Association's president, Andrew Barnes, recently claimed that many law firms view technology as a threat instead of a solution. Although 97 per cent of the association's members have made some kind of investment in technology, 73 per cent believe it is responsible for either a positive or negative change in their firm.

The internet offers a platform for competitors to use non-conventional law firm structures to deliver quality at a lower fee. This recent development is putting conventional law firms under pressure to reduce their costs and increase productivity. Upgrading technology doubtlessly delivers cost benefits and is administratively easier and offers a faster solution than instigating pricing structure reform.

According to Barnes, automating systems and moving manual tasks online is the answer to delivering services at a lower cost with increased responsiveness to the client. Technology, according to Barnes, makes it possible for firms to "compete with people not only in their own town, but across the country, and some of the providers that are crossing international borders."

This Organizational Agility model is based on the earlier work of Rosabeth Moss Kanter—the highly regarded Harvard Business School's management thinker. Kanter believes, as I do, that performance is essentially about speed.

Law firms that turn a blind eye to the realities of the commercial world are playing a dangerous game, warns Barnes. A number of firms have gone out of business across the world already and it is not only small firms that are at risk.

"The current law firm business model is in danger of extinction," states Barnes.

One telling statistic is that medium firms are most content with their progress. Barnes explained that medium firms are more nimble than some of the larger firms in the market space and have the capital to make changes as necessary.

Smaller firms lack the resources to invest in technology and business development and, while larger firms can probably make structural reforms quite easily, mergers with international firms have taken decision-making abroad and prolonged the reform process.[1]

We toss the word *performance* around a lot, especially when it comes to employees and organizations: "He's not performing," "She's increased her performance on the job," "That team performs well under pressure," "That manager needs to pick up his game," and on it goes. We hear and make these sorts of comments all the time. But what do we actually mean? Performance is understandably high on the priority list of business owners, managers, scholars, and management consultants the world over.

But what does it really mean to perform in a transformational global economy? Does it mean exceeding certain KPIs? Is performing at work more than a set of KPIs? What is at the heart of organizational performance? Instead of regurgitating several well quoted definitions of performance from a bunch of reputable sources, I want to discuss agility and its various dimensions and their relevance to organizational performance. Further, I want to introduce a model of agility to evaluate organizational performance.

From the original profit perspective, the evolutionary thinking around organizational performance has been branded as the goal, systems, process, stakeholder, and competing values models. My model fits with the contemporary phase of performance thinking around agility.

This organizational agility model is based on the earlier work of Rosabeth Moss Kanter—the highly regarded Harvard Business School's management thinker. Kanter believes, as I do, that performance is essentially about speed. Speed is characteristic of agility. She originally articulated this link between performance and speed 20 years ago.[2] The only real difference since Kanter introduced her model of speed is that speed is now even more crucial to enterprise success. Speed is synonymous with organizational agility, maneuverability, and flexibility.

What's more, speed, maneuverability, and flexibility are enablers of agility. Conversely, rigid, inflexible organizational policies, procedures, and practices peppered throughout an organization, disable agility. Not being agile limits the organization's speed to adjust, change, or transform to accommodate new and diverse demands. Fluctuations in the marketplace could include anything from new government legislation to an emerging trend in consumer preferences, and everything between. While impossible to predict the future with any confidence or certainty, we understand, as Heraclitus, the pre-Socratic Greek philosopher said, "Change is the only constant in life."[3] So the question for leaders is: *Can we improve our capacity to be responsive to sudden and unforeseen change?* And the answer is *yes*; by being agile.

Kanter cites three types of speed necessary for optimum performance in a warp speed economy. We'll consider these shortly. The organizational agility model includes these three dimensions of speed. I've added four more dimensions to complete the model.

As we discussed earlier in Chap. 2, learning and speed are inseparable. I want to elaborate further on this connection. Learning boosts agility, which then improves performance. Learning builds mastery; learning stimulates our critical thinking; learning broadens our horizons; learning helps cope with complexity and the problems it challenges us with. Learning stimulates agile behavior.

Acute competition, the bewildering array of choices open to the consumer, and the commoditization of goods and services, mean that speed and responsiveness is the difference between the performing and non-performing company. Enterprises prospering in this hyper-competitive global marketplace do things faster than their competitors, with at least the same quality.

As a customer, I want new and better products and services at a good price; swift turnaround time for any "stuff ups," and my preferences met. I'm sure I'm not alone in these preferences. If companies can't—or won't—do all this, then I'm shopping elsewhere, either virtually or actually. So performance is ultimately about speed, and speed comes from applied learning, and the capacity to be agile.

Getting back to Kanter's three-dimensional model of speed, let's take a brief look at three types of speed, before considering four additional dimensions of agility:

- innovation,
- processing, and
- recovery.

Innovation Speed

Innovation speed means being in the marketplace first with new goods and services that customers want and need. Speed in this sense is about constantly experimenting with new features that give customers what they want, before a company runs the risk of losing them to a competitor who is more innovative.

Product life cycles are getting shorter. First-mover advantage continues to become more and more significant for business success. Innovation speed is being agile enough to take advantage of opportunities as and when they arise. An obvious example of innovation speed is *Apple*, and how quickly it got touch screen technology to market several years ago. Although it's common now, it wasn't when the *iPhone* was first released. Being first to market was a colossal advantage to Apple and led to record profits in a short timeframe. Innovation speed can't possibly flourish in an environment where people are trained and rewarded for mindlessly complying with a set of systems and processes. I've plenty to say about the barrier of compliance in Part II.

Innovation is more than thoughts. We've all dreamt of great ideas, only to find someone else putting that idea into tangible affect, and reaping the rewards. So innovation as a dimension of enterprise agility means putting ideas into action to create sought-after products and services faster than anybody else.

We can learn from companies like Apple—noted for its innovation speed. Leaders have to think and operate differently, and persuade employees to do so too. Conventional ideas about performance must be abandoned. The way we use orthodox performance management tools such as the job description and performance review, for example, slows—not speeds up—the capacity to innovate. These antiquated tools box people into work specialties and categories that value obedience above innovativeness.

Processing Speed

Processing speed means dispensing everything through the organization as quickly as possible; faster than competitors. This covers activities such as shortening cycle times for designing training programs, company restructures, and processing products and services from order to delivery. For example, the speedy processing of applications, with appropriate and thorough checks, for approving finances for an investment property may give a banking or finance institution an edge over its competitors. Processing speed is not about cutting corners and forgoing proper QA; it is about getting things done faster, without sacrificing quality.

A company's processing speed can give it considerable advantage over its rivals. Improving processing speed requires everyone to continually question all procedures, systems, and practices that take place in the enterprise. Process speed is accelerated by asking questions like: *Why do we do things this way? Is there a better and faster way of administering this transaction? What is the purpose of this system? Does this process help or hinder outcomes?* This reflective drill isn't common practice in my experience; we tend to accept things the way they are.

A bureaucratically-run business faces inexorable challenges such as overwhelming amounts of paperwork and too many needless and cumbersome systems and processes. This slows down headway; processing speed is sluggish and unwieldly. On the contrary, an enterprise with no bureaucratic baggage inevitably processes information, makes decisions, and completes tasks quicker and is more competitive.

> **Where the rubber meets the road ...**
>
> **Automated phone messages**
>
> Think for a moment about those infuriating automated phone messages we get when we call a company or government department, wanting to speak with a "real" person. The "voice" typically launches into a long-winded set of instructions, all the while encouraging you to go to the organization's website to complete your transaction. You stubbornly refrain from taking that option because you think it will be faster to persevere over the telephone. Big mistake! You subsequently get a 9-option menu to choose from.
>
> By the time you get to option four, you've forgotten what options one, two, and three are. By the time you get to option nine, you get the option to hear all this again! And then, just as you think your query is about to be answered, the voice tells you that "all operators are busy right now; you have been placed in a queue." The automated voice either instructs you to go through this torture again, or tells you that someone (a person, hopefully) will call you back within the next two hours, just as you are about to go into a two-hour meeting.
>
> This is a typical example of very poor customer processing speed, all in the interests of "saving" the costs of employing a customer service representative to take your call.

The above case exemplifies the popularly held belief that using technology is a most efficient and cost-effective means of communication. In the interests of cost-cutting, this misapprehension does the opposite—it costs money with customers fleeing to the competition. With an emphasis on communicating via technology, the human element is devalued. Ironically, using technological solutions can result in increasing—not decreasing—the speed of a process; not to mention generating feelings of frustration. Technology isn't always the answer to speedy communication.

Recovery Speed

Recovery speed refers to the time it takes to respond in rectifying a customer mistake. A fundamental tenet of superior customer service is how quickly a company can put right a mistake made; that is, correct a difficult situation concerning a customer transaction. Customers—if they feel their complaint is being dealt with as a priority, in a speedy manner—are frequently reasonably forgiving. Apart from doing the right thing, holding onto an aggrieved customer and not losing them to a rival business is the objective when it comes to recovery speed.

The need for recovery speed is based on the assumption that mistakes do happen; and when they inevitably do, fixing the error as quickly as possible is the best course-of-action. Recovery speed is often only possible when an employee displays appropriate initiative; a characteristic that's not always valued in the hierarchically-structured organization. This is despite the usual rhetoric from management that we are *customer-focused*.

There are several stumbling blocks to recovering quickly from a customer blunder. One impediment is the way we recognize people at work. Rewards and recognition are generally geared toward "getting it right" the first time, when it comes to dealing with customers. So it's uncommon that swiftly rectifying a customer mistake, such as overcharging or sending out the wrong order, is rewarded.

Worse still, not recognizing the value of recovery speed tacitly encourages unwelcomed behavior. It's not uncommon, for instance, for employees, when inevitable mistakes are made, to cover these up, or point the finger of blame somewhere else. In either case, the employee at fault isn't taking any responsibility for making and fixing the mistake. With extrinsic rewards geared toward following set procedures, displaying initiative in mending a mistake with a customer can be perceived as "risky" by the offending employee. This self-protective behavior makes a bad situation worse, when the priority should be the customer's welfare.

As I've said, speed is an enabler of agile performance. Speed relies on adaptability. Companies that move quickly into action are flexible in how they deploy their workforce (Chap. 4). As I point out later, flexibly deployed workforces exhibit higher than normal instances of innovation, processing, and recovery speed. Furthermore, employees have broader rather than narrower definitions of their work in these enterprises. Employees are versatile; they are encouraged and capable of dealing with varying demands and situations, instead of concentrating on the narrow confines of their job specification (Chap. 6).

Consider Jerry, for example. Jerry is a salesperson in a company selling vacuum cleaners. He prefers to deal thoughtfully and empathetically with a customer complaint, before chasing new business. By having this attitude, Jerry shows a sense of responsibility for his organizational role which goes beyond his sales job. Although selling new product is the main KPI in Jerry's job description, he departs from this by going out of his way to solve problems for the company's customers. Although Jerry's occasionally chipped by his boss for not going out and getting more sales, the adaptability he displays in being attentive to his customers pays off. It turns out to be a better investment of time than looking for new sales leads. More sales eventuate from existing, satisfied customers who have been looked after by Jerry.

As I pointed out in the previous chapter, cross-functional work teams can be another practice in promoting agility. Multi-disciplinary teams counter the pitfalls of functional specialization. These project teams open up cross-functional communication channels and build bridges between departments. Companies that respond quickly are innovative, progress things through the enterprise quickly, problem-solve without unnecessary "red tape", and are usually structured around cross-functional teams. Further, cross-departmental structures bring employees—with disparate skill-sets—together to tackle new challenges or solve existing, company-wide problems. Hierarchical structures, in contrast, slow the pace of decision-making and stifle innovation. But even with these apparent limitations, managers are still too dependent on the traditional hierarchical "org chart" and its focus on specialization.

The reality, however, is that learning, speed, and flexibility are what supports agile performance. These attributes call for fresh thinking about performance. Being agile relies almost entirely on enterprising behavior. Displaying initiative is mostly about ingenuity and prudent risk taking, not relying on a script to follow and striving for precision. This seismic mental shift flies in the face of the conventional idea of structuring work around units of specialization.

Consider the organizational agility model in Fig. 3.1. Four more dimensions of agility have been included alongside Kanter's three-pronged model of speed. Specifically, the other forms of agility included in the model are:

3 Seven Dimensions of Agile Performance

Fig. 3.1 Organizational agility model

- continuous improvement,
- customer responsiveness,
- problem-solving, and
- changing direction.

The model illustrates the interdependency between all seven dimensions. For instance, if a business is *customer responsive*, it's most probably in a state of *continuous improvement* too. Or a business noted for speedy *recovery* from customer mistakes will probably be agile in its *problem-solving*. Each dimension relies on other dimensions to perform with agility.

As I did with the dimensions of innovation, processing, and recovery, I'll briefly describe each of the four additional dimensions in the model clockwise, starting with continuous improvement.

Continuous Improvement

Continuous improvement agility is not the same as *innovation* agility, despite often being discussed together. There's an important distinction between the two dimensions. While innovation is about creating something totally new, continuous improvement is about building upon something that already exists. Well known inventions such as the *Post-it Note*, smartphones, and travel luggage with wheels, for example, are new products.

Continuous improvement is a process of refining something to make it better. Hopefully you can see the difference between innovation and continuous improvement; that's the reason they're represented separately in the model. High-performing organizations, nonetheless, need both forms of agility to prosper.

Business improvements come in many forms. Continuous improvement can, for instance, have an influence on:

- improving quality;
- customer convenience;
- reducing costs to the customer and the business;
- increasing the output of products or services;
- increasing safety;
- meeting deadlines;
- enhancing cooperation between stakeholders; or
- streamlining systems and processes.[4]

Improved products and services—or the systems that contribute to these—are a source of competitive or adaptive advantage. The customer—recognizing value for their money—may remain loyal to a company making prized improvements in products or services. The opposite is true too. No regular upgrades to a product or service quality erodes its value. This tests customer loyalty like nothing else. Consumers have choices; and they can readily and easily exercise those choices when product and service quality stagnates.

There are several barriers to continuous improvement arising from misconceptions about performance. I cover these later in Part II. To be agile enough to be in a constant state of improvement, an organization has to adopt a whole-of-enterprise approach to performance. Briefly, a whole-of-enterprise approach concentrates attention on the interdependencies between units; essentially, it begins with systems thinking, or the systems model of performance (Chap. 1).

But instead, most people management practices are fixated with individual performance. An individual model of performance misses the mark. Systems, processes, and methods of interaction and communication between organizational members are more often than not a secondary performance consideration. KPIs are subsequently geared toward individual—not enterprise—performance.

Also, the concept of work specialization reinforces the idea of a one *right* way of doing things. Professionals in each functional area of the business have their unique and "tried and proven" way of doing their specialist work. These work methods are rarely questioned. So the energies in the functional work environment are directed toward following a set methodology.

For example, there is a certain procedure accountants in the finance department adopt when completing a profit and loss statement. Or salespeople in the marketing department have a precise script they learn and narrate with a prospective customer. The functionally trained employee—operating in a specialized work system—is rewarded for unquestioningly following a set pathway; they'll also be rebuked for deviating off the prescribed pathway.

Specialization breeds myopic thinking—or worse, no thinking! A narrow-minded view and routine patterns of behavior aren't helpful for cultivating a culture of improvement. The upshot of this parochial thinking—founded on a performance system that focuses on the individual and not the system they operate in—is to strengthen an attitude of uncritical acceptance of the ways things are done. It's hardly surprising therefore, that employees working in this culture will automatically accede to work practices as they are taught, before critically reflecting on how they could be done better, faster, or easier. Instead of flexibly deploying their skills-set, the employee completes their work tasks the "right" way—the way they're going to be appraised by management.

Customer Responsiveness

Agility—as I covered in the last chapter—is essentially a customer-driven concept. All seven dimensions of agility impact the customer somehow. The dimensions of *recovery* and *customer responsiveness* are directly related to the customer, and the other five are indirectly related. Since business is dependent on customers, and agility is a customer-centric idea, it's reasonable to include customer responsiveness in the model as a separate dimension.

What's more, an enterprise can be agile, maneuverable, and speedy and still disappoint the customer. In 1956, Peter Drucker, the great management thinker, famously replied to the question, *What is the purpose of a business?* with the following response: *The purpose of a business is to find and keep a customer.*[5] Brilliant in its simplicity, Drucker's response captures the essence of business.

Without customers, a venture isn't a business. Without at least a handful of customers, a business probably won't survive, let alone prosper. So any model of performance—particularly one based on agility—can't ignore the customer as its central focal point. Ideally, everything that is said, thought about, or done in an enterprise should have the customer top of mind. All aspects of a business's operational performance, in other words, should be considered from the perspective of the customer. Producing good quality, value-for-money products or services that are sought-after, in the first step is being customer responsive.

Apart from having something worth selling, customer responsiveness refers to the capability and desire to react swiftly to customer inquiries and requests. Customer responsiveness is a reactive type of agility, unlike, for example, being innovative, which is a proactive behavior. In practice, customer responsiveness is returning phone calls from customers and responding to their email requests promptly, putting customers in touch with the "right" person, and adequately answering their questions and helping them solve their problems. Having the right systems and processes in place helps to react with speed and priority. This is easier said than done, particularly when a business uses out-of-date people management practices, such as restricted communication channels between managers and employees. But the bottom line is this: Show me a thriving business, and I'll show you a business with extraordinary agility in its responsiveness to customers.

The reason customer responsiveness is elusive isn't due to a lack of will on the part of the business owner; it's because of internal barriers caused by performance management traditions. Consider the job description; one such obstacle. The job description is designed to quarantine the employee's thinking and activity around a small chunk of work called a *job*. The concept of the job has been in existence for a little over 200 years. The job-holder often fails to see past their job boundary to think about dealing with a customer's request in a thoughtful, creative way, unless perhaps they have a customer service job. And even for jobs designed to service the customer, being responsive is not as simple as it sounds.

To be truly responsive and agile with customers, a job-holder needs personal qualities like initiative, resourcefulness, and empathy. But the job description typically prescribes a standardized, predictable way of dealing with the customer. A bunch of KPIs generally support this prescribed, depersonalized process. This homogenized approach therefore impedes agile, flexible, and responsive behavior. The mental straightjacket the job description places upon the job-holder is further reinforced by a system of "Pavlovian conditioning."[6] Put another way, the extrinsic reward and punishment scheme is intended to get the employee to follow the perfunctory work document: the job description.

Even when the job description mentions the requirement to be customer responsive, the rhetoric doesn't match the reality. Managers—striving to keep control—favor employees reacting to customers in uniform, expected ways ("Do you want fries with that?"). QA is paramount. Managers fashion and fortify a regulated work-setting, one that is easy to manage, manipulate, and remunerate. Needless to say, this workplace asphyxiates enterprising behavior; the trademark of customer responsiveness.

Notwithstanding these performance inhibitions, today's complex economy and the accelerating rate of transformation puts a premium on enterprise responsiveness. Overwhelmingly, senior executives the world over believe that the ability to anticipate and address the forces affecting the business is critical to business success.[7] So responsiveness—particular customer responsiveness—is an important dimension of agility.

Problem-solving

Workplaces are intricate organisms with an assortment of multi-faceted problems, predicaments, and dilemmas needing solutions daily. Only a few decades ago, workplaces were slower, localized, and predictable. Being able to problem-solve is now part of the repertoire of the sought-after employee. Even though problem-solving is a core skill-set in a multifarious, transformational working world, the performance systems universally used haven't kept pace with change.

The rigid, obstinate systemization of our workplaces daunts people to think freely. This regimentation began deliberately in the early twentieth century with the scientific management movement; it was popularized by the *McDonald's Corporation*'s franchising regime. Against this backdrop, people are told constantly to show initiative at work, but are instead rewarded for being obedient. This paradox is understandably confusing. And most employees—given a choice between being enterprising and compliant—choose the latter. Justifiably, people—in their tightly controlled work environment—front up to work each day on autopilot; they leave their creative and enterprising self at home. People mindlessly follow protocol at work.

This scenario is pretty typical in the majority of unskilled and semi-skilled work-settings in process-driven industries, such as hospitality and construction. Under a schedule of being told *what* to do, *how* to do it, and *when* to do it, workers have minimal leeway for exercising original thinking or thinking creativity. Independent thinking is frowned upon; it can even adversely affect one's career prospects.

I'd like to share a personal experience that perfectly illustrates my point. I recall staying at a five star hotel a few months ago on a speaking tour throughout South-East Asia. Having just had one of the best meals I've ever eaten in one of the four restaurants in the hotel complex, I decided to approach the receptionist after leaving the restaurant and paying my bill. My wife is a magnificent cook; perhaps I should say, chef! At any rate, I wanted to get a copy of the recipe for this superb Thai dish I'd just had the pleasure of eating to take home for Carol.

The receptionist was positively beaming as I approached her in the hotel's grand foyer. I said to her with a great deal of enthusiasm, "I've just had the most magnificent meal in your Thai restaurant and I was wondering if you could do me a favor please?" The receptionist smiling from ear-to-ear replied, "Yes Dr Baker, I would be happy to help you." "Would it be possible for me to get a copy of the recipe for that meal, please?" I blurted out with a copy of the menu clutched in my hand.

The receptionist's demeanor changed instantly and dramatically. Mild panic swept across her face; she went as white as a ghost! The smile vanished into thin air. The receptionist was undoubtedly thinking to herself at this point—*what am I going to do?* I could see that she wanted to dive under the reception desk and look for the procedures manual to tell her what to do in this particular situation. Of course this kind of request wouldn't be documented anywhere. She had to think on her feet, literally. This is an example of a challenging problem that employees face regularly—mostly on the frontline—where there is no obvious solution. After much consultation with the boss, I received the recipe!

Many roadblocks prevent employees from displaying suitable initiative to solve these kinds of predicaments; ones they encounter frequently. Unfortunately, employees aren't generally taught to problem-solve. So, when the employee is confronted by a unique situation that needs resolving, they tend to default to the stock standard answer in the procedures manual; assuming of course there is an answer! They understandably "play it safe." "Sorry sir (or madam), I can't help you. It is not within our scope," is the archetypal inflexible response we've all been on the receiving end of. Problem-solving agility is conveniently avoided, despite its relevance.

Changing Direction

The agility to change direction is a culmination of the other six dimensions:

- to *innovate* is to change direction;
- to *process* faster requires a change in normal practice;
- *recovery* from a mistake means changing direction;
- *continuous improvement* is about altering the way something is done;

- *customer responsiveness* is usually about shifting priorities to cater for the need of a customer; and
- *problem-solving* is often about thinking outside the box.

Agility is ultimately about changing direction in some form.

Even so, I felt it important to separate the dimension of changing direction from the other six. Operating in a climate of accelerated change and uncertainty, being able to change direction is critical to performance. All enterprises need the agility to change direction rapidly in response to unanticipated changes in the marketplace. These variabilities may involve the emergence of a new market, such as building a housing estate to accommodate an influx of miners to an area next to a new mine site. Or, it could be a change of government and new priorities and laws, such as reductions in immigration intakes. Or, changes in economic conditions, such as a sudden downturn in economic activity, can have severe and sudden impacts on revenue in the tourist or entertainment industries. All of these ups and downs require companies to reassess their strategic direction and make agile adjustments in riposte.

Without an agile direction shifting capability, a business faces two serious problems: First, the firm misses a potentially lucrative, passing opportunity that suddenly emerges because it's too slow to capitalize on the sudden opening—or worse, not being able to change at all. Second, a company entrenched in its customs—perhaps too comfortable in its existence—will become redundant in no time. Consider the following examples: *Kodak*; the local independent hamburger shop; and the local butcher. But being flexible and maneuverable isn't quite as easy as it might sound; like the other six forms of agility, there are obstacles.

Take for example the belief that leadership is about offering *certainty* and *clarity* to those they lead. This common conviction can be a problem when dramatically altering a business's direction is necessary. Because it's so deeply engrained in our psyche that leaders are there to provide clarity and certainty, managers look for ways to emulate this belief. Leaders continually strive to develop and communicate a comprehensive strategic plan, for example, to offer "certainty" to employees and shareholders.

But the concept of the *five-year plan* is an artefact of the twentieth century. Apart from being completely unrealistic, the strategic plan makes it tough to rationalize taking a different route. The manager—having invested considerable time and thought in the initial plan—finds it hard to let go of it; the strategic plan then becomes "a rod for the back" of the organization.

A sudden, unplanned direction change implies that management has miscalculated the strategic route in the first place—which is probably the case. Managers lose face by contemplating a direction about face. Not wanting to admit fault or appear incompetent, the manager may be tempted to stay the original course. So a golden opportunity may pass by.

A more suitable leadership approach is shifting from linear planning to a strategy of *adaptive leadership*.[8] Divergent thinking or opening up the array of possible futures is the essence of modern leadership. Contingency planning is more suited to the transformational marketplace. Preparing for multiple scenarios can replace the illusion of certainty that strategic planning used to offer. Linear planning, at any rate, is the antithesis of agile direction change.

This brings us to the end of Chap. 3 and Part I. I've covered the seven dimensions of agility that make up the organizational agility model. Agility is the new way of evaluating organizational performance. There are, however, several people management practices that make enterprises clumsy rather than agile. These obsolete practices need to be overthrown to accommodate agile performance. A complete rethink of performance is warranted.

I intend to discuss these performance roadblocks in detail in Part II, and offer some practical alternative solutions. More specifically, Part II of *Performance Management for Agile Organizations* deals with eight management myths we have entertained for a 100 years, many arising from the scientific management movement beginning in the early part of the twentieth century. These eight myths are both pervasive and constraining for the agility needed for work in the twenty-first century.

Chapter 4 considers the first myth—*Job specification improves performance.*

The Top 10 Key Points …

1. This chapter introduces and defines the organizational agility model of performance.
2. This Organizational Agility model is based on the earlier work of Rosabeth Moss Kanter, who claims that organizational performance is inextricably tied to speed.
3. Speed is synonymous with organizational agility, maneuverability, and flexibility.
4. Innovative speed means being in the marketplace first with the goods and services that customers want and need.
5. Processing speed involves dispensing everything through the organization as quickly as possible.
6. Recovery speed refers to the speed it takes to respond to a customer problem satisfactorily.
7. Continuous improvement agility is improving on something that already exists.
8. Customer responsiveness is the agility of reacting to the needs of the customer.
9. Problem-solving agility is about solving problems, predicaments, and dilemmas.
10. The dimension of changing direction is a culmination of the other six dimensions of agility.

Notes

1. Nelson, F. (2014). Firms slow to change with the time. http://www.lawyersweekly.com.au/news/15588-firms-slow-to-change-with-the-times
2. Kanter, R.M. (1995). Mastering change. In S. Chawla & J. Renesch (Eds), *Learning organizations: Developing cultures for tomorrow's workplace* (pp. 71–83). Portamd, OR: Productivity Press.
3. http://www.ask.com/world-view/said-only-thing-constant-change-d50c0532e714e12b
4. Baker, T. (2013). *The end of the performance review: A new approach to appraising employee performance.* London: Palgrave Macmillan.

5. http://www.peace-university.net/25040.php
6. https://en.wikipedia.org/wiki/Classical_conditioning
7. Economic Intelligence Unit (2009). *Organisational agility: How businesses can survive and thrive in turbulent times.* London: Economic Intelligence Unit.
8. Adaptive leadership is a practical leadership framework that helps individuals and organizations adapt and thrive in challenging environments.

Part II

Myths Blocking Agile Performance

4

Management Myth # 1—Job Specification Improves Performance

When I left school as a "baby boomer," my parents encouraged me to consider an occupation where I could specialize and so have job security. Their reasoning was well-intended, simple, but misguided: If you can find a niche where you can use a specialized set of skills, you can define a market segment for yourself. This line of thinking was predicated on the stable and relatively predictable, preglobalized marketplace. The logic of my parent's argument no longer applies; the rules have fundamentally changed.

I vividly recall an actual conversation with my father about my career options in my senior year of school. At the time, I had no idea of what I wanted to do with my life. As an aside, I've always admired 16 or 17 year olds who have a crystal clear idea of what they want to do with their lives. It can be a stressful and uncertain time for young people and their parents. Although I was more interested in humanities than the sciences, my parents suggested I consider optometry.

"Optometry is a specialized area. People will always need glasses and you'll be safe in that field," said my father, with some conviction. "You need to find

---

Specialization breeds a "paint by numbers" mentality: *This is how we do things. We've always done things this way. If we follow the system we'll be successful.* These statements portray the prevailing assumptions of specialization.

© The Author(s) 2017
T. Baker, *Performance Management for Agile Organizations*,
DOI 10.1007/978-3-319-40153-9_4

a specialty; something that is secure and will be around forever. At some stage in everyone's life, they need glasses," Dad continued, justifying his statement.

My father's argument made sense to me at the time. However, I wasn't particular excited by the thought of working in the field of vision care. Optical laser surgery became possible a decade after our conversation. People now have the option of correcting their eyesight by surgery, instead of purchasing a set of spectacles or contact lenses. It's little wonder, then, that optometrists are diversifying into other areas, such as selling sunglasses.

A specialized profession with a seemingly secure future is not quite as sheltered now as it once was. But like most professions and occupations, diversification and the flexible deployment of a skills-set is the new reality.

Many optometrists, for instance, have flexibly deployed their professional expertise to offerings beyond vision care to include the diagnosis and management of ocular disease.[1] This has been part of a decades-long trend to enlarge optometry's scope of practice and to maintain or grow revenues lost to companies specializing in laser surgery and dispensing eye wear.

My father was right in one sense: The optometry profession has evolved and protected itself by expanding into other areas of health care; but it's being done through flexible deployment, instead of specialization.

In the following eight chapters of Part II, I focus on eight beliefs that negatively impact a business's capacity to exercise the agility they need to prosper. Each chapter is structured in the same way. First, I define the dysfunctional thinking and practice holding business back from performing with agility. Second, I illustrate the link between current practices and scientific management, or what I sometimes refer to as *Taylorism*.[2] Third, I explain how the practice dulls agile performance. Drawing on the Organizational Agility model defined in Chap. 3, I cite the dimensions hampered most by the misguided management belief. Fourth, I propose a better option to replace the dysfunctional practice. These proposed practices are all approaches diametrically opposite to those used in scientific management. Fifth, I share some application tools characterizing the new approach and illustrate how it aids agility. And finally, I reflect on the results of using these practices and tools.

So we begin with the concept of *specialization*.

In a business context, specialization is a common differentiation strategy. Finding a niche market and dominating it with focused knowledge, products, or services has been a highly effective competitive strategy for over a century. Since the 1980s, marketing gurus have preached the competitive advantage of specialization. Similarly, the employee has been told the same thing: Develop a specialized skills-set and apply it in a particular field to retain job security.

There are numerous illustrations of successful companies electing to specialize, such as lending institutions specializing in home loans, construction companies specializing in commercial property, and so on. But there's a downside to operating in a niche market. A business striving to corner a specialized market may sacrifice their scope for agility. These companies are inclined to replicate their external strategy, internally. More specifically, the enterprise segments and organizes itself around functions or specialized clusters of activity. This division of work is not dissimilar from the *Ford Motor Company* assembly line 100 years ago. The organizing of people around specific functions—while doubtlessly efficient—creates challenges for flexibility, adaptability, and responsiveness.

One of the agile performance barriers is the job specification. The practice of erecting clearly defined boundaries around jobs makes sense on the surface. Job specification is designed with the purpose of controlling the work of the employee; to make them accountable for a set of clearly defined tasks. So what's the price to pay for this clarity and accountability?

A smart and agile enterprise has three characteristics, I think, when it comes to its labor force. First, it has a highly skilled workforce. Second, there is a high degree of flexibility within that workforce. And third, the employees are in a continual state of honing and improving their skills. Job specification impedes these fundamentals; in particular, the last two characteristics. The inherently inflexible job specification can, for instance, slow internal mobility. Learning skills outside the explicit limits of the employee's job description is not encouraged, and even discouraged. These limitations raise a question: *Can an enterprise achieve the three characteristics of an agile workforce and—at the same time—reap the benefits of job specification?*

An alternative approach—*flexible deployment*—doesn't necessarily abandon job specification altogether. Flexible deployment means the employee accumulates a range of skills and competencies outside the scope of their job specification. In short, they have a broader skills-set. In practice, flexible deployment doesn't, however, necessarily entail becoming a *jack-of-all-trades*; it isn't about transitioning from a specialist to a generalist.

Through the flexible deployment of their skills-set, the employee is capable of appreciating and understanding a bigger scope of operational activity outside their job boundaries. The systemic deployment of competencies across the enterprise, leads to better organizational adaptability and maneuverability. Being more adaptable and maneuverable contributes to greater responsiveness, increased speed, and more agility.

More on that later. But first, we need to understand specialization and its origins.

Job Design and Scientific Management

Scientific management was the genesis of job design. Specialization has its origins in Taylor's scientific management philosophy. Taylor broke the assembly line up into a series of specialist tasks and treated each component separately in his analysis of how performance could be boosted.

The driver for specialization was waste minimization and efficiency enhancement. By identifying the best way of performing a task, wastage in time, resources, and effort is abated. Taylor studied each job in the factory to determine the least amount of time and effort required to complete it. So standardized methods of performing a job was central to Taylorism. Each job on the assembly line would be meticulously planned in advance, and employees were paid to perform particular tasks in the way specified by management.

So the present-day people management practice of *job specification* originated from Taylor's job specialization. A job specification entails breaking down a job into its simplest component parts and assigning them to a job-holder to perform the tasks in a consistent and efficient manner. There are several obvious advantages to designing work around a job specification. Breaking tasks into small elements, with clearly defined repetitious processes, lessens the skill requirement of the job itself. It also decreases discretionary effort in the execution of the tasks and therefore reduces costs. Training timeframes are short and standardized, recurring tasks are broken into simple parts, and the success of the learning experience is likely to be high. But job specification, as I've alluded to, has drawbacks.

From a motivational perspective, breaking a job into small, repetitive, and simple component parts can make the work dull and repetitive. Boredom can lead to negative consequences such as higher than normal levels of absenteeism. A job specialization can be ineffectual in environments that are dynamic and unpredictable. In these volatile work-settings, the workforce needs to adjust its approach in response to the demands of the situation. Selling products or services in cross-cultural environments, for example, requires extensive agility that can't necessarily be documented as a generic process in a job specification. Despite these shortcomings, specialization puts the onus on the manager to be accountable and the job-holder for achieving outcomes.

Taylor's philosophy of scientific management paved the way for automating and standardizing work, virtually universal in today's workplace. The concept of the assembly line—where each worker performs simple tasks in a recurring fashion is Taylorism in action. Job specialization eventually found its way into service industries too. One of the biggest success stories of the application of scientific management principles, as I mentioned in Chap. 3, is the McDonald's franchise operation. McDonalds were the first fast-food restaurant to incorporate the divisions of specialization; one person takes the orders while someone else makes the burgers, another person applies the condiments, and yet another wraps them. With this level of efficiency, the customer generally receive a product or service with reliable quality.

So if specialization can be applied successfully in McDonald's restaurants, and is now a feature of many fast-food franchise systems, how is it problematic from a performance standpoint? Specialization, as I've described it, encumbers adaptive behavior. Job specification hampers several dimensions of agility. More specifically, specialization adversely affects the dimensions of innovation, recovery, continuous improvement, customer responsiveness, and changing direction. Apart from being repetitive and dull—and the impact that has on motivation levels—fully engaging people in this type of work can be hard. I consider this more fully later in Chap. 8. But for now, let's concentrate on the main performance problem of specialization: it stifles agility.

An employee having the innovation mindset I spoke about in Chap. 2 is going to be frustrated if confronted with an endless procession of standardized processes and procedures to follow, for instance. In a segmented and process-driven workplace, questioning the *status quo* isn't valued to the same extent as following the *status quo*. What's more, the concept of specialization implies the specialist "knows best." Specialists are inclined to obediently follow established practices. If a completely new method is advanced in a procedure-driven environment, it infers the "old" system is somehow inferior or substandard. This idea isn't always easy to accept; the current situation in most cases is defended vigorously and the proposed method rejected.

The speed of recovery from a mistake—such as overcharging a customer—usually requires a flexible response from someone in the offending company. But a strict, process-driven workplace can inhibit unorthodox replies to an error, no matter how sensible it may appear. Employees—when mistakes are made—understandably default to the apparent safety of following stock-standard approaches, as we discussed in the last chapter. The dimension of continuous improvement is less of a problem, however. Innovation though, is challenging in a workplace segmented into specialists. Nevertheless, implying a need for improvement suggests the established system is broken in some way and that—as I say—is difficult to accept.

Being truly responsive to a customer's need requires agility, as we've discussed; and being agile is essentially about trying new approaches when a situation warrants it. Specialization breeds a "paint by numbers" mentality: *This is how we do things. We've always done things this way. If we follow the system we'll be successful.* These statements portray the prevailing assumptions of specialization. For example, McDonalds took a long time—many would say, too long—to change direction and introduce "healthy" food options onto its menu. Changing direction is harder when a business is made up of a series of specialized methods and processes to produce its goods and services.

Although a job specification is an effective way of holding a jobholder accountable for the work they're supposed to do, it is ineffective at promoting agile behavior. Specialization breeds "tunnel vision;" the employee cannot—and doesn't necessarily want to—understand or appreciate the way the rest of the organization operates. This blinkered thinking is designed to get the employee to focus all their energies on a few, manageable work tasks to a required standard.

So, let's return to flexible deployment as an alternative to specialization. Can it work in tandem with specialization?

Flexible Deployment

The practice of flexible deployment is essentially about utilizing an employee's skills and abilities in a variety of roles and work situations. There's little doubt the employee—working in the transformational global marketplace—needs to learn and apply a wider range of skills to maintain their relevance. For this and other reasons, flexible work approaches are quite common in the changing workplace. But as a people management practice, flexible deployment isn't usually implemented in a systematic way; or for the proper reasons. Applied in a coordinated fashion, with the right motives, employing skills-sets in a comprehensive range of work situations, increases the employee's and organization's capacity to operate with agility.

Three key things are essential for successfully instigating a flexible deployment program. First, all employees—not just a select group—undergo training and coaching in areas beyond the scope of their current job specification. Second and aligned with learning and development, a multi-skilling program needs to be implemented in a coordinated and systematic way. This program commences within the employee's immediate team first, and eventually spreads to cross-functional learning and application. Third—to gain full buy-in from the workforce—an incentives program encouraging employees to progressively learn new skills and capabilities should accompany the learning process. These three characteristics are the essence of a strategically planned program of skills deployment across the business.

But in reality, organizations that are based on specialization have no discernible link between their learning and development program and flexible deployment (Chap. 10 for more about this). The majority of training, after all, is designed to support the specialization of job skills. People—not to mention the organizations they work for—are deprived the opportunity to fully develop if training programs are restricted to current job specifications. Employees and organizations consequently fail to cultivate skills and competencies in the range necessary to cope in the relentlessly transforming work-setting. And if a multi-skilling program does exists in these traditional workplaces, it's often used to cut employment costs. The conservative thinking behind this cost-saving measure is: *If we can train people to do a variety of tasks, we can reduce the number of employees and cut our labor costs.*

If the principle motive behind introducing flexible labor strategies is to cut operating costs, then one of the costs that's likely to be cut is learning and development. In businesses adopting this approach, the responsibility for skill development rests squarely on the shoulders of the individual employee. Managers with a cost-cutting mentality may introduce flexible deployment strategies as a means of slashing the business's training budget and its obligations for developing the people working in it. While this isn't an unusual practice regrettably—justified on the basis of reducing costs or "overheads"—it isn't the right rationale for carrying out a policy of flexible deployment. In the long run, slashing the learning and development budget can cost more money than it may save in the immediate term.

Beginning any form of flexible work arrangement is based on the goals of management. Flexible forms of work shouldn't be used as a cost-cutting strategy, however. But my research indicates that the flexible deployment of labor, in many cases, is synonymous with deregulating the workforce and reducing the costs of employment.[3] Enterprise flexibility however, doesn't necessarily mean deregulating the workforce. It certainly doesn't mean that cutting employment costs will improve the agile performance of a business. Promoting agility in all its dimensions should be the sole purpose of practicing flexible deployment.

Besides its rationale for implementation, the implementation itself is not always done well. It appears we have some way to go to positively apply flexible deployment programs in organizations. Take for example some recent research conducted by the Chartered Institute of Personnel and Development (CIPD) in the United Kingdom. The results indicate that only 28 per cent of employees surveyed believe that the training provided by their organization is relevant beyond their immediate duties, with 27 per cent concerned about whether their skills will be relevant in the future. Finding time for training is another concern for employees. CIPD's research indicates that 39 per cent of employees say they can't find time to undertake training and development programs. Other apprehensions are costs associated with these training programs and the less than positive interest levels of employees to be involved in these programs.[4] It is therefore of little surprise that specialization remains the dominant practice in industry and there are several impediments in breaking this mould.

Notwithstanding the prevalence of specialization, there are several effective strategies of flexible deployment. The most used practices are *job rotation*, *job enrichment*, *job enlargement*, and *multi-skilling*. I'll concentrate on multi-skilling here, and provide a practical tool for easy and effective implementation. By focusing on multi-skilling, I'm not suggesting other people management practices don't have merit; they do. But in the context of promoting agility, I think multi-skilling can get the best results in the quickest time, with the most people.

> **Where the rubber meets the road …**
>
> **Benefits of multi-skilling**
> United Kingdom food producer *Campbell's Grocery Products* wanted to make the most of their technicians' skills using the flexible deployment strategy of multi-skilling. The company recognized that its 20 technicians—10 per cent of the total workforce—were underused. Their role was to work on the production line, helping operators, and come off the line to repair breakdowns. But their on-line duties prevented them from practicing their skills. All 20 technicians were subsequently trained in both electrical and mechanical skills to attain a multi-skilled standard required. This was done over two and half years. Most of the training was delivered internally, on site, during each technician's shift. The results were quantifiable: stock accuracy improved, the levels of surplus stock held in the warehouse fell, the number of breakdowns reduced, customer response times shortened, and the time taken to repair faults decreased. Simultaneously, technicians' morale and team spirit greatly improved, especially as a result of the increased efficiencies generated by the training, which resulted in less "firefighting" and frustration. The technicians' former feelings of irritation were replaced by feeling that they were contributing to the site's success.[5]

Skills Matrix

One of the most effective ways to systemize a multi-skilling program is via a *skills matrix*. This is a simple yet effective tool for coordinating a multi-skilling and retraining program for all employees. Starting with all teams, the skills matrix can then be used within each department, and eventually across the organization. Its implementation for smaller firms is more straightforward. To be clear: Before looking at cross-functional flexible deployment, all employees should be exposed to a variety of skills within their immediate team first. After demonstrating mastery of several skills and tasks within their team, employees can then embark on acquiring competencies in other areas of the business.

I should point out that not all tasks are open for multi-skilling. In large enterprises, this would be impractical anyway. However, wherever possible, an attempt should be made to ensure that more than one—and possibly several employees—can perform each organizational activity to a minimum required standard. It stands to reason that the more multi-skilled the workforce is, the more agile the organization becomes in the deployment of skills. The employee benefits too: the more skilled and employable they become. This is a "win–win" situation. Or, if you consider the consumer as well, you might refer to this as "win–win–win."

To coordinate and monitor this flexible deployment process, each team within the company creates their own skills matrix. A skills matrix can be defined as the breakdown and recording of all the tasks necessary—and open to multi-skilling—for the unit to function and achieve its purpose. The first step then, is to identify the range of tasks, roles, or competencies required within that particular team's bundle of activities. Once this has been done, the second step is to assess the skill level of each employee against those tasks. Step three is to coordinate a coaching program for all team members so they can become multi-skilled beyond their immediate job specification. These three steps are done across the organization at the same time for each team.

The old adage: *What gets rewarded gets done* is true. To supplement this multi-skilling process, and to encourage a flexible learning culture, each employee should receive some form of incentive for mastering a predetermined number of skills, beyond the scope of their current job description.

Table 4.1 illustrates a simple skills matrix.[6]

4 Management Myth # 1—Job Specification Improves...

Table 4.1 Skills matrix

Team member/Competency	1	2	3	4	5	6	7	8	9
Joe									
Mary									
Bill									
Harry									
Sue									
Kathy									

Legend

Trainer
Competent
Undergoing training
Not yet trained

Six employees are shown in the skills matrix in a specific team in a business. For instance, this could be a team in marketing, accounts, or production. Numbers 1 to 9 along the top of the matrix illustrate that there are nine core tasks, roles, or competencies required within that team. White spaces on the matrix, signifying "Not yet trained," represent competencies that require training for that particular team member. For instance, Joe requires training in competencies 6, 7, 8, and 9. In other words, this skills matrix indicates that Joe has yet to be exposed to any learning of these competencies.

Light grey spaces on the matrix ("Undergoing training") signify competencies where the individual has had some training or coaching, but has not yet achieved a consistent minimum acceptable standard of performance without close supervision or coaching. For example, Joe has commenced training in competency 1 in the matrix, but isn't yet competent.

Dark grey spaces ("Competent") represent tasks where the team member is competent. For example, Joe has achieved mastery in competency 5. Competency in this case can be defined as having achieved a consistent minimum acceptable standard of performance on the job; the employee is able to complete that task in an unsupervised capacity.

Black spaces ("Trainer") identify individuals who have achieved competency and have been delegated the task of coaching their fellow team members in that competency. For example, Joe is qualified to coach his fellow team members in competencies 2, 3, and 4. To qualify as a workplace trainer or coach, that individual must have certain qualifications and attributes. As a reasonable starting point, they must have reasonably good communication skills, have achieved and demonstrated competency in that skill area, and completed a foundation "train the trainer" type program.

As pointed out before, a rewards and incentives program should be linked to the learning and the skills matrix. Using the above example, Mary is the most multi-skilled of the six employees within the team; she has achieved competency in five task areas. So, from a skills acquisition point-of-view, she is currently the most valuable—and, arguably, most crucial—member of the team. She therefore qualifies for some form of reward or incentive for learning and applying these new skills. Also, Joe, Bill, Kathy, and Mary are the only employees in that team who have qualified to coach their colleagues in two or more tasks.

In a medium sized or large organization, once all the teams within a department or functional area have a flexibly deployed workforce, the next step is to formulate skills matrixes throughout the department. A new skills matrix can then be developed and implemented across team boundaries and include cross-team competencies. The primary objective is to facilitate multi-skilling within each department of the business. Once this second phase of the multi-skilling program has been achieved, a similar process can be repeated cross-functionally, or between departments. Eventually—through this process—the organization will have greater agility to exercise its workforce. This practice shifts the emphasis from specialization to flexible deployment.

I'm not suggesting we completely abandon the job specification. After all, as a people management practice it has several benefits we've covered in this chapter. To recap, a job specification does the following:

- lets people know what is expected of them in their core job duties;
- makes it is easy to regulate individual performance; and
- keeps the job-holder and their manager accountable for achieving specified outcomes.

But the job specification has its weaknesses too; most notably, it reduces individual and organizational capacity for agile decision-making. I've suggested applying the practice of flexible deployment to enhance agility and boost the business's adaptive advantage in an increasingly competitive global marketplace. The use of the skills matrix is suggested as a simple and powerful multi-skilling tool. If the employee is held accountable for their job specification on the one hand, and the deployment of their skills in various work situations on the other, they're bound to benefit, and so too the business.

This brings us to the end of Chap. 4. I want to move now to the second dysfunctional practice that negatively impacts organizational performance. It is based on the myth that *quality systems and processes guarantee good outcomes.*

The Top 10 Key Points …

1. From a business perspective, specialization is a common practice of differentiating from competition. Finding a niche market and dominating it with focused knowledge, products, or services has been a highly effective business strategy for over a century.
2. The present-day people management practice referred to as a job specification originated from Taylor's job specialization characteristic of scientific management. A job specification entails breaking down a job into its simplest component parts and assigning them to an employee to perform the tasks in a consistent manner.
3. A job specialization is ineffective in environments that are rapidly changing or unpredictable. In these volatile work-settings, employees need to adjust their approach according to the demands of the situation.
4. In a segmented and process-driven workplace, questioning the *status quo* is not as valued as following it.
5. One way of stimulating agile behavior is flexibly deploying employee skill-sets within a business.
6. Flexible deployment means the ability to transfer and apply skills and competencies across a wider range of tasks than those in an employee's job specification.

7. Beginning any form of flexible work arrangement is undoubtedly based on the goals of management. Flexible forms of employment shouldn't be used principally as a cost-cutting strategy.
8. One of the most effective ways to systemize a multi-skilling program is via a *skills matrix*.
9. Wherever possible, an attempt should be made to ensure that more than one—and possibly several— employees can perform each organizational role or task to a minimum required standard.
10. Applying a skills matrix throughout an organization shifts the emphasis from specialization to flexible deployment.

Notes

1. Smick, K. (2015). What does the future look like for independent optometry? http://www.eyecarevof.com/blog/2015/5/22/what-does-the-future-look-like-for-independent-optometry
2. "Taylorism" is named after Frederick Taylor, considered to be the main architect of scientific management.
3. Baker, T. (2009). *The 8 values of highly productive companies: Creating wealth from a new employment relationship*. Brisbane: Australian Academic Press.
4. Zheltoukhova, K. (2014). HR: Getting smart about agile working. CIPD research paper.
5. Baker, T. (2009). *The Eight values of highly productive companies: Creating wealth from a new employment relationship*. Brisbane: Australian Academic Press.
6. Baker, T. (2014). *Attracting and retaining talent: Becoming an employer of choice*. London: Palgrave Macmillan.

5

Management Myth # 2—Quality Systems and Processes Guarantee Good Outcomes

Mary was becoming more and more frustrated. Her bank decided to stop a special arrangement she had with her previous bank manager. This arrangement allowed Mary to undertake certain transactions expeditiously. This arrangement was different, however, to standard bank policy. Due to the bank lacking a system to record such an arrangement, Erica, the new staff member refused to honor Mary's previous arrangement with her bank manager.

When Erica refused to process her request, Mary demanded to speak to the branch manager. Erica chose to speak with her supervisor, Stan, instead. Stan also said no, claiming it was against bank policy. This was despite Mary's assurances that she had an arrangement in place.

Increasingly aggravated, Mary pressed for the branch manager's name and email address. After some discussion, she was eventually given those details.

Mary subsequently fired off an email to Stephanie, the branch manager, explaining the problem, requesting reconfirmation of the previous arrangement and a method of recording the decision. The email also demanded the name

---

Despite the emphasis on the customer, quality is assessed, ironically, not by the end-user but by whether or not the organization has met certain internal criteria. And if so, the organization gets the literal seal of approval by a regulatory body for meeting industry standards. And if not, the organization forfeits its QA certification. The customer isn't consulted.

and email address of a higher-level manager, should Stephanie choose to refuse her request.

To Mary's surprise, Barry, a relief branch manager, responded, as Stephanie was on vacation. Barry's reply did not address Mary's concerns, and again stated the standard bank policy. Further, Barry responded by giving Mary the customary freephone number for the customer relations department and a website address to lodge complaints.

Even more frustrated, Mary demanded the details of the manager of the customer relations department. Having emailed the manager, Sergio called Mary. However, Mary was in a meeting and so Sergio left her a message. Mary called back at the conclusion of her meeting and was told by a recorded message that she had called outside regular business hours, which were between 9:30 a.m. and 4:30 p.m. Mary had called at 4:40 p.m.

Mary's frustration turned to anger. She again asked for the contact details of someone interested in her feedback. The head of customer relations, Jan, finally called Mary back. They had an extensive discussion, but Jan was unable or unwilling to change the bank's position. However, Jan did give Mary the name and contact details for the area manager, Ross.

Mary called Ross and they had a discussion about her situation. Ross still wasn't willing to allow Mary to have her own way. However, Ross was concerned that Mary had been unable to speak directly with her bank manager, and he promised to put a note on the file for Mary's unusual transaction arrangement.

Rebecca, the branch manager, returned from vacation. Mary rang the call center again; she couldn't get through to the branch. Rebecca rang back on Monday, but missed Mary, leaving her number. Mary called back, and the call went straight to the branch (hooray!).

It took two minutes for Mary to discuss the issue with Rebecca and for her to reinstate Mary's agreement. To complete the transaction, Mary went to another branch. She stated that she had a special arrangement with the branch, the teller looked it up, found the details, and successfully processed Mary's transaction.[1]

The second myth—*quality systems and processes guarantee good outcomes*—is the central justification for the QA movement. As an organizing system, QA gained momentum after its initial success in the early stages of scientific management. After a brief overview of QA and its evolution, I consider the impact Taylorism has on quality and its supporting beliefs. With lots of affirmation—and little criticism for the most part in the management literature—QA is hardwired into the psyche of management. But it has deficiencies for cultivating a culture for agile performance, principally when it comes to developing the customer-focused attitude essential for the current economy.

The challenge fundamentally boils down to balancing the necessity or producing high quality goods and service with a flexible and adaptable approach. Being customer-focused sounds simple. But customer-focus requires a multi-faceted strategy. A sizable portion of the strategy goes further than relying on superior internal QA systems. Customer responsiveness—one of the seven dimensions of agility—is more than producing and distributing superior products and services.

The Origins of QA

The concept of quality didn't start with scientific management. But Taylor elevated the status of QA by demonstrating its significance to organizational performance. Taylor's principle idea was this: By analyzing the component parts of work, one could determine the most efficient and effective way for those work tasks to be accomplished. So scientific management was the beginning of the modern QA system. Also, Taylorism shaped managerial responsibility to safeguard that the work of employees be done in a set way. Employees too, were—and still are—made responsible for following a prescribed process for completing their work. So Taylorism was the genesis for what we have now come to know and accept as QA, and the associated roles and responsibilities of managers and employees.

Product quality and process control, however, date back thousands of years. The idea of process controls began with the building of the pyramids of Egypt, when a system for quarrying and dressing stone was designed. Later, Greek architecture would surpass Egyptian architecture in the systems it used. Centuries later, the shipbuilding operations in Venice introduced elementary production control and standardization. Following the Industrial Revolution and the birth of the factory system, quality and process control began to take on some of the characteristics we use today.

Specialized labor and quality assurance took a giant leap forward in 1911 with scientific management; it has had a profound influence on management thought and practice ever since. Taylor's philosophy was one of extreme functional specialization; he recommended having eight functional bosses on the factory floor, one of whom was responsible for product inspection. Taylor's ideas of process analysis and quality control inspection of the final product are still with us today in many firms. Statistical quality control, the forerunner of today's TQM or total quality control, had its origins in the mid-1920s in some companies.

During World War II, W. Edward Deming and Joseph Juran separately developed the TQM versions we use today. It's generally accepted that the Japanese owe their post-war product dominance to applying Deming and Juran's TQM philosophy. United States industry ignored their contributions for 40 years and has only relatively recently converted to statistical quality control. During the 1980s, the concept of "company quality"—with a new focus system management—came to the fore. It came to be accepted that if all departments approached quality with a consistent and committed approach, success was possible from management leading the quality improvement process. As we know, QA isn't limited to manufacturing; it's now applied in all forms of business or non-business activity. This includes design, consulting, banking and insurance, computer software development, retailing, investment, transportation, education, and other industries and business activities. The QA industry infuses organizational life in every way, shape, and form.

Despite its omnipotence, what in essence is QA? There are myriad definitions of QA. But in broad terms, QA is perfecting the way things are done to produce quality products and services to meet the needs and expectations of the end-user: the customer. The practice of QA has developed to include progressively more phases of work and will doubtlessly continue to evolve. Anyhow, the execution of QA is the systematic process of monitoring and evaluating the various aspects of work to maximize the potential for advancing and maintaining high standards of quality.

Early twentieth-century industrialists adopted an engineering approach to management. Taylorism called for the careful analysis of tasks and time-and-motion studies in conjunction with piece-rate pay schemes to improve productivity. Adherents of this method searched for the "one best way" to perform a specific task, and introduced standard procedures. Taken to its extreme, scientific management identifies the single best way to perform work-related tasks and activities.

The Shortcomings of QA

Taylor's approach to quality has been widely criticized for several good reasons. One criticism is the time, effort, and subsequent cost associated with developing these work standards. More specifically, resources are devoted to closely monitoring standardized methods in many different aspects of production, and calculating fair rates of pay for completing these tasks as prescribed. The costs of doing all this may offset the benefits gained from the practice.

Another problem arising from the scientific management of quality is the predictably strong resistance from those doing the work this way. This resistance is largely due to the attempts by management to closely measure effort and productivity; what we might now refer to as "micromanagement." Employee autonomy and freedom of choice about how to do the job at hand gave way to control and restriction by management. This process model of performance we raised in Chap. 1, doubtlessly leads to eroding individual initiative and reducing motivation with the repetitious doing of rudimentary tasks in the *one best way*.

The counter argument to these shortcomings is this: By following a set of well thought out systems and processes, the customer is virtually guaranteed of receiving a quality product or service. As an illustration, if you buy a "Big Mac" in any restaurant in the world, you get a burger that pretty much tastes the same, has the same packaging, the same ingredients, and even at a similar comparative price. Briefly, QA promises that the customer gets what they pay for.

Despite the emphasis on the customer, quality is assessed, ironically not by the end-user, but by whether or not the organization has met certain internal criteria. If they have, they get the literal seal of approval by a regulatory body for meeting industry standards. And if not, the organization forfeits its QA certification. The customer isn't consulted. Under the QA regime, the customer is relegated to a secondary consideration. So it's somewhat paradoxical, isn't it, that meeting the customer's expectation was the original driver behind Deming and Juran's concept of quality and specifically, TQM?

Speaking of customer expectations, these have been influenced by technological advancements and the intensification of competition. What's more, the consumer's idea of quality has changed too as a result of these factors. In the food industry, for example, people's concerns about food safety, health, animal welfare, and environmental factors are more prevalent now than at any time in history. So safety, health, animal welfare, and environmental protection are issues affecting quality in food quality. Putting it another way: Food quality is being evaluated on factors other than taste, availability, service, and price.

Rather than getting the proverbial "tick in the box" for meeting industry standards, performance also hinges on understanding the business's customers and their evolving expectations.

Let me be clear about this: QA is—and will probably continue to be—an important dimension of producing quality products and services. I'm not suggesting we do away with QA. The main thrust of my argument is that we need to balance QA considerations with a focus on the customer. QA and customer-focus aren't necessarily the same thing. QA isn't the complete solution to meeting the customer's perception of quality. It's part of the answer, albeit an important part; but not the only part.

It ought to be said that QA practices now extend beyond the physical gates of the business. QA includes supply chains and how stakeholders are communicated with, for instance. All facets of the business, both internally and externally, have a QA system attached to it. Although, the concentration of activity is still very much around in-house operations. Smart, responsive, common sense, adaptive behavior can get overlooked in the quest for across-the-board standardization.

Getting the Balance Right

Customer-focus, as I define it, can't be accomplished through QA measures alone. So what's the *right* balance? How do we strike this balance between quality control and agile performance? What does it mean for a

5 Management Myth # 2—Quality Systems and Processes...

company to be truly customer-focused? As we both know, you and I are more demanding as customers than our parents; we have a greater array of options open to us; we expect value for money; and we take into consideration when purchasing beyond quality assurance.

Micah Soloman, author of *High-Tech, High-Touch Customer Service*,[2] identifies six major trends transforming the way customers expect to be treated. First, we want instant gratification; which means we want the right information literally at our finger-tips from a smartphone. Second, there's a noticeable shift to values-based buying. According to *PricewaterhouseCoopers*, 87 per cent of United States consumers believe companies should value societal interests at least as much as their own business interests.[3] Third, there's an appreciable greening of the customer; younger customers, mainly, have concerns about the environmental impact of the products and services they consider purchasing and consuming. Fourth, as customers we look for timelessness: products and services that are authentic and long-lasting. Fifth, we want to be empowered in our purchasing decisions; we expect companies to respect us; to make it easy for us to contact them when we need to; and for the business to respond to our feedback promptly, thoroughly, and thoughtfully. Sixth, as customers we have a growing desire for self-service; fueled by our round-the-clock, tech savvy lifestyle; the desire for self-service choices, from online shopping to concierge-like touchscreen menus in public spaces. These six developing trends illustrate the need for product producers and service providers to be flexible and customer responsive as much as anything else.

To be performing with agility means that products and services and the way they are accessed, delivered, and packaged must be constantly under review. A company like *Kellogg's*, for example, is always developing new breakfast cereals. But the challenge for Kellogg's is more than developing new brands; to be successful on an ongoing basis means the company needs to get their pricing right to cater for customers who have an ever-increasing array of brands and pricing to choose from. This requires creative ways of promoting their products, using a range of marketing channels such as competitions, product tasting, and distribution. QA is one of several other systems and practices that contribute to a successful and popular breakfast cereal.

If a company is captive to the process model of performance only, their goods and services will disappoint the customer eventually. Being customer-focused is more than producing consistent quality in goods and services. A customer-focused business is one where decisions about its products and services are made on the basis of a continual alignment with the wants and needs of the customer and the overall goals of the enterprise. As I said in Chap. 3, being customer-focused in essence involves everything said, done, and thought about by all organizational members having the customer in the forefront of their mind. This attitude is the starting point for agile performance.

> **Where the rubber meets the road ...**
> **Thinking outside the box**
> *Southwest's* senior vice president for corporate communication, Ginger Hardage, told participates at a conference a story about a Southwest pilot:
> "On September 11, 2001, after terrorists had brought the twin towers down, all planes that were already in the air were grounded. A Southwest plane was directed to land at an airport that Southwest did not serve, and the passengers and crew were put up in a hotel. When Southwest management called the hotel to enquire about the passengers and crew, they were told that no one was there—the pilot had taken everyone from that plane out to the movies."
> "There's no manual from which to learn that," said Hardage. "At Southwest, employees are encouraged to make decisions from the heart, and in turn, these proactive gestures provide positive benefits to the customers and the company."
> A recent survey showed that 76 per cent of Americans think that a company's treatment of its employees is a major factor in whether customers will purchase from that company. As Southwest makes its employees the top priority, Southwest is really making its customers come first, too.[4]

The Customer-Focused Enterprise

Customer-focused enterprises are nimble; on the one hand, they honor their QA system and use clear, simple, and practical processes to accomplish their many tasks and activities. On the other hand, the business is agile, adaptable, and flexible enough to change direction in response to the ebb and flow of the marketplace. This duality is synonymous with

5 Management Myth # 2—Quality Systems and Processes... 81

the competing values model of performance I discussed in Chap. 1. To reiterate: The three main competing values-sets are internal versus external, flexibility versus control, and process versus outcome. Being able to successfully accommodate these polar opposite values is one way of evaluating organizational performance. It's also the basis for the customer-focused enterprise.

Being a customer-focused enterprise means being ambidextrous. The quality systems used are characteristic of internal, controlling, and process-driven values. An external, flexible, outcome-driven set of values supports the other dimension of the competing values model of performance. The agile employee is a problem-solver who can see past a blind adherence to organization policies and processes. It's not that they are disobedient and disrespectful of company protocol. The agile employee endeavors to juggle company needs for standardization and orthodoxy with customer needs.

To illustrate this juggling act between pleasing the customer and satisfying the business, consider the salesperson's role. People who work in sales are the "meat in the sandwich." They are crammed between two important and demanding entities: company and customer. Further, salespeople have two bosses: their manager and their customer. Conflict arises when the manager and customer have different expectations about a product or service. A conflict can be based on a number of issues including price, delivery, or after-sales service. In these difficult circumstances, the salesperson has four options:

- satisfy their manager at the expense of the customer;
- please the customer at the expense of their manager;
- try to satisfy both the manager and the customer; or
- disappoint both!

In this case, the customer represents the external, flexible, outcome-driven dimension. And the boss is the custodian of the internal, controlling, and process-driven dimension. The salesperson is in the middle.

This dilemma isn't limited to people working in sales and customer service; it affects a growing number of employees. As businesses become leaner and resource strapped, greater numbers of employees within the company deal directly with customers. Employees in technical roles such as engineers, tradespeople, and accountants, for instance, work closer to customers and clients than previously. Those people paid to work directly with customers have a more extended set of responsibilities than in the past. Salespeople are more involved than they once were in after-sales service matters. And the opposite is the case too. Employees in customer service roles are now expected to promote and sell other products and services during their customer interactions. So more people are caught up in this brokerage role between the organization they work for and its customer-base.

But in the main, salespeople and customer service representatives are brokers between the company and its customers. So in their boundary-spanning role, employees working directly with customers are agents who are frequently forced to negotiate organizational needs and customer expectations. This would suggest that as employees in this role, they require considerable managerial support.

To help with the burdens of this brokering role, managers should invest time and resources assisting employees coping with this dual demand. Also, the customer-focused employees must be willing to be adaptive and learn when and how to display appropriate initiative and enterprise; in other words, be agile. It's in everybody's interests to strive for this customer-focused attitude, and not just default to playing it safe by following internal policies.

But how is this achieved in practice?

There are four managerial strategies to support customer-focused behavior. First, the employee needs to have a clearly understood role. This role clarity builds their confidence to deal with the inevitable conflict between the competing demands of the customer and the company. Second, a consistent, fair, and valid incentives system for desirable customer-focused behavior needs to be applied for all employees within the business. Third, a comprehensive, well-implemented, and easy-to-use customer relationship management (CRM) system captures and utilizes important information and data to make informed customer decisions. And fourth, all staff are exposed to tailored, timely, and relevant customer service training and coaching, based on real-life scenarios. With a QA system in place, these four practices are the factors that balance two sets of competing values: a compliance-driven organization and a customer-focused enterprise.

Three additional elements are important too. An effective internal customer service culture—based on the systems model of organizational performance—removes in-house barriers. These obstacles are usually a result of the specialization practices we covered in the last chapter. There needs to be a commitment from management to adequately invest in technical and administrative resources, and people development practices. This obligation helps to create a smooth and responsive customer interface. And finally, all of these initiatives need committed and sustained leadership.

The majority of books on customer service concentrate on how employees should interact with customers. Little is said about the bigger picture; that is, what needs to be done to cultivate a customer-focused culture. These books don't usually devote much time to overcoming the competing values of compliance and adaptability. Instead, many of these books talk about putting systems in place to improve customer responsiveness; that is, the emphasis is on QA and the internal-focus.

Also, there's not a lot written about the challenges of rewarding and recognizing good customer-focused behavior. Perhaps this is because it's complex. First, how do you reward someone fairly and consistently for great customer-focused behavior? How do you ensure that the reward is suitable? Just knowing where to begin is difficult enough. For instance, should someone be rewarded for following the system or accomplishing a great outcome? It's easy to suggest both, but then how does a manager ensure that the reward is commensurate with the deed? Second, you have issues around the implementation of rewards: Where and when to start, and how often and how much? Though by not recognizing exemplary customer-focused behavior, leaders send a signal to the "troops" that the company isn't seriously focused on the customer.

I'd suggest a good place to start addressing these questions is through a cross-functional project team. Invite the team to consider how the organization ought to respond to these issues and ask them to report their findings. When this has been done, I've usually been pleasantly surprised by what comes back.

In any event, recognition before reward is the easier of the two incentives. One of the simplest, most effective—and often neglected—ways, for instance, of recognizing exemplary behavior is to mention it during regular staff meetings to acknowledge the effort publicly. If time is set aside at meetings for saluting commendable customer work, the leader is recognizing and reinforcing this kind of behavior.

Furthermore, I'd suggest trying this approach: At regular meetings, start on a positive note. Ask each person for an instance of customer-focused behavior they've observed in the previous fortnight. Not everyone will be that observant, but some will have examples to share. This exercise can be insightful, and sends a strong signal about the leader's priorities. Although this simple form of recognition doesn't answer the questions I pose around rewards, and specifically, their consistency and reliability, it's a good starting point.

Dealing with out-of-the-ordinary customer demands is another challenge not dealt with adequately in the management literature. These "left field" requests require more than good negotiation skills. The qualities needed in these unique situations are many and varied. For instance, the employee needs to

- be a team player,
- have a depth of experience,
- be empathetic,
- appreciate the implications of the request on colleagues, and
- be open to being flexible and adaptable.

These are only a few of the traits needed. There are doubtlessly many others I've missed. Nevertheless, bundling someone off to a one-day customer service training course is not the answer to dealing with unusual customer requests.

Instead, drawing attention to these unique requests is useful. Using exceptional customer demands as a learning opportunity, can be very helpful. *How could we deal with this situation in the future, if it happens again? What are the important lessons learnt here?* These are two great questions for discussion internally. Regrettably, managers use the excuse

5 Management Myth # 2—Quality Systems and Processes...

they're too busy dealing with the next crisis to spend the time learning from these incidents that are nuggets of learning.

Yet another challenge is the limited career paths for people working in sales and customer service. Usually, there isn't a defined career path for these employees. Vertical promotion in these roles is comparatively limited. Plus, the prevailing wisdom is that to advance to general management, a person needs exposure in several areas of business. These career limitations often result in good people with ambition moving on and leaving the company, looking for other opportunities. High turnover isn't unusual in sales and customer service. And loyal customers—not to mention the company—are often left in the lurch when this happens. Retention of good staff in sales and customer service is an issue for lots of businesses. The answer to this predicament lies with the flexible deployment practices we spoke about in the last chapter.

And finally, there's often significant resistance to sharing valuable customer-based information across the business. This can be especially problematic when extrinsic rewards don't favor information sharing. I came across such an example and wrote about it in one of my previous books, *Attracting and Retaining Talent*.[5]

A well-known international commercial retail travel agency I consulted with was concerned about a lack of teamwork among travel agents in the retail outlets. They wanted me to "fix" the problem. I asked the managing director how he rewarded his staff. He told me that at the end of each month a table was published with each agent's name and the value of sales they had made during the month. Bonuses are paid on the basis of these figures. "Can you see the problem with this bonus system?" I asked. So determined were these travel agents to improve their sales figures, they wouldn't share useful information with others.

Once he'd accepted this dilemma, this managing director cited an example of a salesperson "stealing" a lead from a colleague's desk, while they were out to lunch. The salesperson decided to call the customer and book the flight for them in their colleague's absence. Not mentioning this to their colleague, the person who had "taken the initiative" was credited with the sale. The individually-based reward system worked against teamwork in this, and many other cases in the business.

To be customer-focused, I'm not suggesting we neglect QA. Like the other seven dysfunctional practices, QA is only dysfunctional to the extent that it interferes with an enterprise's ability to be agile. The QA industry has proliferated. Virtually everything in business is now subjected to QA. Scientific management—as much as anything else—paved the way for our modern version of TQM. The modern employee is taught to follow a system or process for pretty much everything they do at work. This obedience mentality can asphyxiate initiative and enterprise. The customer and their heightened expectations require more than compliance, however. Despite QA being driven by a focus on the end-user, the practice has overtaken its original aim. Organizations need to be ambidextrous: they must be able to comfortably accommodate the competing values of control and enterprise.

This is the end of Chap. 5. In Chap. 6 we look at the third myth: *The job description helps the employee understand their organizational role.*

The Top 10 Key Points …

1. The second myth—quality systems and processes guarantee good outcomes—is the prevailing philosophy of the QA movement.
2. The concept of producing quality didn't start with scientific management; but Taylor elevated the status of QA by demonstrating its significance to organizational performance.
3. In broad terms, QA is perfecting the way things are done to produce quality products and services to meet the needs and expectations of the end-user: the customer.
4. Despite the emphasis on the customer, quality is mostly measured by whether an organization has met certain criteria; if so, they get the literal seal of approval for meeting industry standards by a regulatory body.
5. QA is not the total answer to focusing on the customer; it is part of the answer, albeit an important part, but not the only part.
6. The developing trends illustrate the need for product producers and service providers to be flexible and customer responsive as much as anything else.

7. A customer-focused business is one where decisions about their product and services are made based on continually aligning customer needs and wants with the overall goals of the company.
8. People in sales and customer service positions, in particular, are in a brokerage role between the organization they work for and customers they service.
9. With a QA system in place, there are four practices that move the company from a compliance-driven organization to a customer-focused enterprise.
10. A common challenge that's not generally considered in the management literature is how to deal with out-of-the-ordinary demands of the customer.

Notes

1. Baker, T. (2014). *Attracting and retaining talent: Becoming an employer of choice*. London: Palgrave Macmillan.
2. Solomon, M. (2012). *High-tech, high-touch customer service: Inspire timeless loyalty in the demanding new world of social commerce*. USA: AMACOM.
3. Parisi, C. (2013). What is customer service? 6 major trends changing the customer's expectations. http://playbook.amanet.org/what-is-customer-service-6-major-trends-changing-the-customers-expectations/#.VinmjrKxJvQ.email
4. Baker, T. (2009). *The 8 values of highly productive companies: Creating wealth from a new employment relationship*. Brisbane: Australian Academic Press.
5. Baker, T. (2014). *Attracting and retaining talent: Becoming an employer of choice*. London: Palgrave Macmillan.

6

Management Myth # 3—The Job Description Helps the Employee Understand Their Organizational Role

The longer an employee works in a company, the more likely it is that they assume responsibilities beyond their original job description. What's more, as the employee climbs through the ranks, chances are that they have job duties that aren't replicated elsewhere in the company.

Take Margo, for example. Margo began in an entry-level accounting position 20 years ago in a large firm. When new computer accounting software was adopted in her department, she took an active role in the transition from the old to the new system. Margo worked closely with the IT department to configure the new platform to accommodate the needs of the company. She has coached all new and existing employees in the new software package since its adoption. Margo, in preparation for her retirement, developed and documented a training program to use the software.

The company is now looking to fill the void Margo's imminent retirement will create in the accounting department. The selection panel came to the conclusion that no one employee would likely have the unique skills-set neces-

---

Overall, the job description has served industry well; the employee has a clear blueprint to work from and the manager is given a frame-of-reference to manage the performance of the employee. But the transformative changes from industrial to knowledge work has rendered the job description far less useful than it perhaps once was.

© The Author(s) 2017
T. Baker, *Performance Management for Agile Organizations*,
DOI 10.1007/978-3-319-40153-9_6

sary to assume all of Margo's job responsibilities. In fact, no one—least of all, the selection panel—is really sure what all of Margo's job responsibilities are now; they certainly aren't covered in her original job description.

Jennifer, Margo's manager, suggests that the first step is to find out what Margo actually does on the job before trying to find her replacement. A work document is put together that details as best as possible Margo's evolved tasks and responsibilities. Using this new job description as a reference, the company decides to divide the position into three parts: accountant, technology liaison, and trainer. From this point, the company decides how to fill the vacancies created by Margo's retirement in the following ways:

- *A new entry-level accountant will be hired.*
- *A veteran accountant will take on the additional duty of being the liaison between the accounting and IT departments for technical matters.*
- *To prepare for a planned expansion of the accounting department, following a recent corporate acquisition, a designated trainer will be hired to train the employees in the company's technology gained from the merger. The company expects that the new trainer will also be an asset to other departments in future endeavors.*

Margo will transition her responsibilities to her successors in the coming year in preparation for her retirement, following a predetermined employee development plan for the incumbents. By the time she retires, Margo's successors will be adequately prepared to tackle their new responsibilities and will aid the company in its upcoming expansion. Everybody wins![1]

The concept of the job description grew out of the practice of specialization I covered in Chap. 4. The job-holder is responsible and accountable for a segment of the overall work done by the company. And since scientific management chopped the assembly line into bit sized pieces, the job description became a natural extension of job specialization. From here, the job description has become the backbone of all the major people management practices in organizational life. But the pervasive influence of the job description holds organizations back from exercising agility and maneuverability for performance. Specifically, the heightened awareness of the importance of non-job roles in performance and their relevance in exercising enterprising behavior, don't figure prominently—if at all—in the job description format. A shift from a job description to *role description* broadens the scope of performance beyond the technical requirements of the job.

Overall, the job description has served industry well; the employee has a clear blueprint to work from and the manager is given a frame-of-reference to manage the performance of the employee. But the transformative changes from industrial to knowledge work has rendered the job description far less useful than it perhaps once was. Non-job roles, understandably, aren't usually covered in the job description. But non-job behavior is increasingly important for agile performance. I'm suggesting a role description is a better performance management tool to capture these non-job behavioral expectations; it extends the idea of performance past the technical execution of work.

I've a lot more to say about the job description in one of my previous books, *The End of the Job Description*.[2] But for the moment, I'd like to concentrate on the performance barriers the job description constructs. I'll refer to six common performance management practices hamstrung by the job description. Figure 6.1 illustrates these six familiar practices.[3]

I'll briefly touch on each of these practices shown in Fig. 6.1, and explain how the job description has a negative impact on performance management.

Recruitment and Selection

Amongst several relevant documents, the job specification is the primary reference point for evaluating the best candidate to fill a vacant job. Questions used in the interview process are commonly framed around the job specification document—the mainstay of the job description. The successful candidate is normally the person scoring highest on the job specification criteria. But as we've come to realize, the successful candidate isn't always the right choice. We can all think of a person who "on paper" is more than technically proficient in carrying out the requirements of a job. But later—much later, when it is usually too late,

```
┌─────────────────────────────┐
│   Recruitment & selection   │
└─────────────────────────────┘
              ▼
┌─────────────────────────────┐
│          Induction          │
└─────────────────────────────┘
              ▼
┌─────────────────────────────┐
│    Training & development   │
└─────────────────────────────┘
              ▼
┌─────────────────────────────┐
│         Remuneration        │
└─────────────────────────────┘
              ▼
┌─────────────────────────────┐
│ Succession planning & promotion │
└─────────────────────────────┘
              ▼
┌─────────────────────────────┐
│      Performance review     │
└─────────────────────────────┘
```

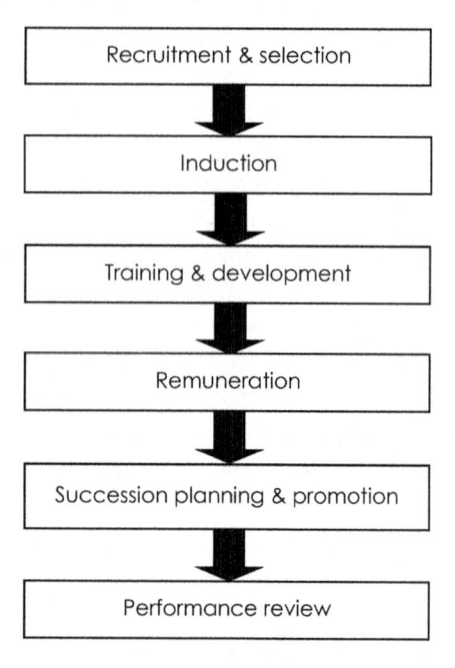

Fig. 6.1 Performance management practices

sometimes two or three months on-the-job—that technically-proficient employee disappoints in areas not cited in the job description.

For instance, their poor attitude and lack of enthusiasm can prove problematic. Or their inability to work constructively with a variety of colleagues and stakeholders may be a serious stumbling block. Or their lack of readiness to continually grow and develop their skills-set could be a liability. Or their unwillingness to offer suggestions and constructive ideas for improving the workplace can be found wanting. Any of these non-technical deficiencies can be costly to the business and the employee.

To illustrate my point, after the probationary period lapsed, Lisa—one of the selection panelists—turns to Rod, another on the panel and says, with a rueful expression, "If only we had known that Bill (the new employee) would treat everyone with contempt and disrespect when we interviewed him several months ago." "If only!" repeats Rod with a sigh.

So these and other important non-job capabilities aren't always taken into account during the selection process. And when they are, they're a peripheral consideration after the technical requirements of the job are thoroughly scrutinized. Yet non-job performance (and non-performance) has a significant bearing on speed, adaptability, and flexibility, and other important agility factors. By judging the worth of a candidate's suitability for a job solely on the limits of the job specification, we aren't taking into account significant capabilities needed for agile business performance. The job description limits our conclusions to technical competency. Non-technical capabilities aren't really taken into account.

Induction

During the on-boarding process, there is usually a strong emphasis on preparing the new employee for their new job. There's less emphasis placed on preparing the employee for their non-job roles. This induction further entrenches the partiality in the selection process on performing job tasks before anything else. From the early stages in the induction process, the new employee can be forgiven for thinking that performing non-job roles is comparatively inconsequential. Not reinforcing the value of non-job roles in the induction practice is a missed opportunity. The newly recruited employee is at their most receptive; they can be shaped and molded to develop new productive habits—or at least—break old, unhelpful habits.

But alas, this starting phase of a new job isn't fully utilized to discuss and agree upon expectations that are not job-related. Although a good leader will make the time to discuss their beliefs around non-job behaviors with their new employee, in the first few weeks, this practice is unfortunately the exception rather than the rule. Instead, the early interactions between the boss and new recruit are usually exclusively involved with on-the-job activities. This initial task-specific dialogue further strengthens the impression in the mind of the new employee that the non-job roles people play at work are less relevant.

Training and Development

Once the job-holder passes their probationary period, they're given training and development opportunities to build their technical skills. Nearly all these training and development opportunities are designed to improve the employee's current and future job competencies. Training programs that build non-job competencies—such as team development, creative thinking, and emotional intelligence—although more widespread than previously, are ancillary considerations to learning technical skills. Training to improve job-specific competencies is still the main approach to organizationally-sponsored employee development.

Training with a technical orientation aids the job-holder to develop their skills-set to do their job tasks with more capability. It's been this way since the birth of industry. Taylor's emphasis on specialization, and his *one best way* approach, amplified the relevance of technical training. There's no doubting the necessity of technical training.

But surviving and prospering in a rapidly transforming economy means that companies need to do more than build technical capacity. There are unique problems, challenges, and dilemmas employees face regularly, where procedural knowledge and skills learnt on a training course can't be applied. In other words, there's not always a convenient, clearly defined "cookie cutter" process to resolving the increasing array of complex problems employees are frequently bombarded with. Solutions to these predicaments aren't always found in the company manual or the technical training curriculum; they require original thought and initiative.

The hyper-competition and unpredictable external environment has elevated the value of solving distinctive and perplexing problems and displaying resourcefulness, often on the spur of the moment. This is unlike the relatively stable and predictable marketplace of the twentieth century. This landscape can be neatly summed up with the acronym: VUCA. VUCA stands for *volatility, uncertainty, complexity,* and *ambiguity*—characteristics of the modern world we live in, and are familiar with.[4]

Personal attributes necessary to navigate the VUCA environment are outside the scope of the job description. Being agile, flexible, and creative, for instance, are some of the non-job-specific qualities of the successful twenty-first century employee, apart from their technical job skills. The job description relegates these personal attributes to the fringe and they are consequently not valued as highly as they ought to be.

I'll have more to say about training and development in Chap. 10.

Remuneration

It's never—and never likely to be—a straightforward exercise to assess the pay levels of employees. Evaluating pay rises is customarily done by using the criteria of job competencies contained in the job description. By sticking strictly to the criteria in the job description, we're deluded into believing our decisions about assessing pay levels is fair and objective. The conventional wisdom is that it's too risky to stray beyond the six to eight Key Result Areas (KRAs) in the job description, when making judgments about employee pay. Other factors, apart from the job description, are therefore overlooked and not taken into consideration. These other attributes are thought to be too subjective.

The consequential belief that managers are objective decision-makers is that they avoid taking into account non-job roles in remuneration considerations. So attributes like being an insightful critical thinker, for example, are not relevant to pay considerations. Taylor thought that pay levels should be linked to the skill mastery. The continuation of this view a century later discourages—not encourages—agile behavior.

So, non-job attributes are regarded minor in the gauging of pay levels. Non-job capabilities such as the following are not openly factored into remuneration decisions:

- a positive mental attitude,
- the ability to work in teams,
- a readiness to continually develop oneself, and
- a willingness to contribute to the efficiency and effectiveness of the workplace.

What's more, managers are disinclined to raise any of these non-job roles during the remuneration interview. The manager doesn't want to "muddy the waters" by raising matters that are not directly related to the task-based KPIs in the job description. The employee too, in their remuneration interview, is reluctant to promote their non-job contributions, knowing they probably won't have any bearing on a pay rise.

The truth is substantially different, however. Non-job behaviors have a significant impact on work performance. Just because non-job contributions (or lack of contributions) are difficult to quantify, doesn't mean they are necessarily any less important. Consider, for example, a work colleague positively exercising their non-job roles can make worthwhile contributions such as:

- *elevating* morale and improve the organizational climate in their surrounding work-setting;
- *contributing* to building better teamwork;
- *developing* harmonious and productive working relationships;
- *upgrading and improving* systems and processes;
- *applying* newly learnt skills and *acquired* knowledge for the benefit and betterment of the work unit.

Such attributes are necessary for adaptive performance.

Succession Planning and Promotion

Talent management is the process of identifying and targeting valued employees for succession and promotional opportunities. This process is based on a succession plan for the future. "Succession planning is the practice of identifying and developing people in the enterprise with the potential to fill key business leadership positions in the future."[5] The job description has insalubrious control on succession planning decisions. The choice of who replaces whom in the event of an incumbent vacating a position invariably comes down to technical mastery. Yet again, non-job performance is not factored into these decisions to the extent it ought to be. The bottom-line is this: The planning of succession boils down to finding or grooming an employee with the same or similar job skills-set.

And it's usually the case that the employee selected to succeed the incumbent is chosen from the same functional area; most likely the next level down in the organizational hierarchy. Although this scenario is understandable, the succession process doesn't always take into account more than the job dimension.

Here is an example of what I mean. Consider succession planning for leadership positions. Going from a technical to a leadership position requires a fundamentally different set of skills; in reality, the two skill-sets are polar opposites. For starters, the technical role is task-related and the leadership role is people-related. An operational job is about doing the work, which requires a certain technical competency. Conversely, the leadership position is about getting the technical job done with and through other people. The widely accepted characteristics of a good leader are to motivate, communicate, influence, delegate, and coordinate. Nevertheless, all industries habitually promote people to managerial positions based on their technical prowess and know-how. The overreliance on task-specific information contained within the job description is the single biggest reason for this deep-rooted practice. If you consider, as I do, that leadership capability is critical for performance success, this practice is nonsensical.

Performance Review

During the traditional annual or biannual performance review interview, managers usually confine their appraisal to the technical aspects of the employee's work. The manager's focus is mostly about whether the jobholder has met their job-related KPIs in their job description. The cost of sticking stringently to the letter of the job description in the appraisal process is that other essential behavior outside the realm of the *job* gets by-passed or—at best—referred to transiently.

Also, countless employees across all industries—even though it isn't always warranted—receive fair, or even good, evaluation ratings at performance review time. This is attributable often to a lack of attention paid by the manager to the employee's non-job behavior. Many "average" or "above average" employees demonstrate substandard, or even appalling, non-job conduct.

Take, for instance, the "toxic" employee—the one everyone tries hard to avoid in the office. Based on an assessment of their technical competence, these employees can pass their appraisal with flying colors. Take another example: The person who has stopped growing and learning and refuses to up-skill, multi-skill, or any skill! This deficiency can be forgiven, overlooked, or ignored if the manager observes the employee successfully achieving their KPIs. These negative non-job performance traits are often disregarded and consequently poor behavior is silently reinforced at appraisal time. What's more, there's no pressure or incentive for the employee to change their inappropriate and non-productive behavior. The result of these circumstances can be disastrous; the organization suffers, the employee's colleagues, their manager, and the employee themselves are impaired too.

> **Where the rubber meets the road ...**
> **Every job has three job descriptions**
> Every job has at least three job descriptions: the company's (the written one on file), the boss's (rarely the same), and the employee's (the one that describes what he or she actually does). In an ideal world, they would all be the same.
> But in the real world, they aren't the same, and that causes a lot of problems. When perceptions differ. Consider these challenges:
> Hiring becomes a game of chance—hire to the wrong job description, and you're not getting a good match for the job.
> Evaluation and appraisal become confused—measured goals don't reflect actual challenges and accomplishments.
> Compensation makes no sense—it's based on erroneous assumptions.
> Productivity suffers—confusion abounds about duties and responsibilities.
> **What causes job description mismatches?**
> The three-job-description scenario arises from several factors:
> *Jobs change*
> For example, adopting newer technology may affect a job dramatically. Take a job that once demanded split-second decision-making. Now the computer makes those decisions. Does the job now require a less-skilled worker? Maybe. Maybe not. It might now require computer programming skills.
> *Products and processes change*
> The product itself can change, or the equipment or process used to manufacture it can change. That might make the job easier or more difficult to perform; it might also create or eliminate a need for special knowledge.
> *Physical surroundings may change*
> A change in the job's physical surroundings might affect the level of hazard or fatigue, creating the need for protective garments or equipment and/or creating a need to accommodate an otherwise qualified individual in the job.

> (continued)
>
> *Bosses may not know what their people do*
> There's often a disconnect between what bosses think their employees do and what the employees actually do. Maybe you can't blame the boss too much—everyone's overstretched these days.
>
> *Employees don't always do what they are told*
> It's not unusual for employees to do whatever it takes to get their jobs done, no matter what their job descriptions say. For example, one may have a job description that describes the job as "final assembly and packaging," but the realities of the job are that the real challenge is cajoling other departments to get their portion of the order ready.
>
> As another example, new technology may not work well, so employees tend to do their jobs "the old way." The bosses think the expensive upgrades have changed the nature of the work, but the employees just pay lip-service to the technology and use their old systems to get the work done.
>
> **Three job descriptions or one?**
> Whatever the causes of job description confusion, it's HR's job to get the three job descriptions to match. How can you go about this?
>
> First of all, set up a formal review program that requires job descriptions to be reviewed regularly, perhaps at annual review time, or three months before annual review. Both boss and employee should complete a review.
>
> Second, put some teeth into the requirement. Make it part of the boss's appraisal.
>
> Third, keep an ear and an eye out. Observant HR people will detect the situations in which people are not doing what their job descriptions say they should be doing. Get out on the floor; talk to people; see how things are going. When you find something amiss, get with the boss and fix it. Soon enough there will be just one job description for each job.[6]

Performing at work goes well beyond the piece of paper we refer to as a job description. I've explained how six common people management practices are adversely influenced by the job description. And because of its pervasive presence, the job description severely distorts the non-job dimension of work to irrelevance in managing performance. This is even though we instinctively understand the value of these attitudes and non-job behaviors. Furthermore, it's these non-job roles that propel the business toward the adaptive advantage I've spoken about.

And it's also worth mentioning that we use the job description to justify sacking someone; it provides legal protection for the disgruntled manager. While managers use non-adherence to content in the job description as the basis for termination of someone's employment, ironically it's dreadful non-job behavior that's more often than not the real reason for dismissal. There's no doubting the omnipotence of the job description; it guides and informs every aspect of the employment cycle, ranging from recruitment to termination.

So what's the substitute for the job description?

Non-Job Performance Framework

I think the answer lies with elevating the significance of several universally relevant non-job roles in the milieu of employee performance. The job description is the wrong tool for doing this, for the reasons I've outlined. In a nutshell, I'm suggesting replacing the job description with a role description.

Indeed, non-job-related performance criteria has to have the same rigor applied to it as the job-specific role. I understand that some organizations have what they call a *role description*, which generally amounts to a list of bullet points as an appendage to the main task-focused document. I've yet to see non-job roles spelt out in the same detail as the KRAs, KPIs, and targets in the job description document. Non-job roles are generally expressed in vague statements such as: *We encourage employees to offer their suggestions at work*; or perhaps more directly: *You are expected to be a team player*. Either way, non-job role descriptors—if they are included at all—are inevitably listed after the task-specific job details, toward the end of the document. There's an absence of detail and how they will be measured and so they are open to misinterpretation.

And it is with these paucities that I'm promoting a broader interpretation of employee performance; one that goes further than the job-specific behaviors of the traditional job description. The non-job performance framework supports and reinforces desirable workplace accomplishment that isn't job-specific. What's more, I want to overhaul the key deficiency in the performance management system—the job description—and replace it with a role description that covers both the job and non-job roles.

Figure 6.2 illustrates this more expansive framework of work performance.[7]

The job description covers the *Job role*, *KRAs*, *Competencies*, and *KPIs* illustrated on the left-hand side of Fig. 6.2. In the role description, the job is conceptualized as the *Job role*. The arrangement on the right-hand side, consisting of *Non-Job roles*, *Elements*, *Competencies*, and *KPIs*, is related to non-job behaviors. In effect, this means that the role description consists of five roles: one job role and four non-job roles.

There are four non-job roles in the framework, which are undoubtedly becoming increasingly significant in any agile workplace:

- positive mental attitude and enthusiasm role
- team role
- career development role
- innovator and continuous improvement role.

There are unquestionably many other roles—apart from the four in my framework—that contribute to personal and organizational success. But these four roles are undeniably applicable in all industries and work contexts.

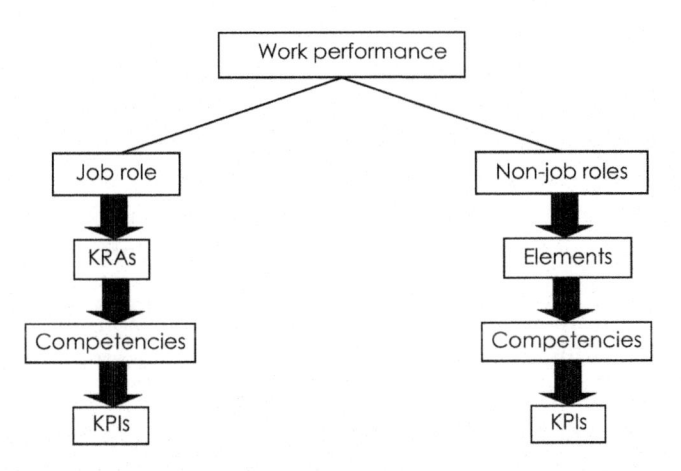

Fig. 6.2 Model of work performance

Two of the roles in the framework are *interpersonal* and the other two are *personal*.

Interpersonal Non-job Roles

I'll define the positive mental attitude and enthusiasm role first. It is impossible to be positive and enthusiastic all the time at work, or anywhere else for that matter. But equally, it would seem that being negative and lacking enthusiasm all the time is impossible too. Although I have met some people that test this proposition! Everyone's attitude affects those close to them. And that's why I've categorized this role as interpersonal; though one's attitude is a personal choice.

I think it's reasonable to expect everyone working together in an organization to retain—most of the time—a positive mental attitude and enthusiasm. Research shows that enthusiasm and a positive attitude is the highest rating attribute managers look for in employees.[8] With the considerable pressures on organizations to repetitively and rapidly "chop and change," being positive is essential for building and upholding morale through these relentless adjustments and disruptions that can be demoralizing.

Employees and their managers have for some time been expected to "do more with less" and this adds another layer of pressure on the working environment. Throw in: intensified competition, the snowballing fixation in "dotting i's and crossing t's," and the burden of accountability and transparency regiments, all heighten stress levels exponentially. Maintaining an attitude that is positive can be an antidote for these pressures and stresses; cultivating a harmonious working environment is a priceless commodity today. So it's unsurprising with all these 360 degree stresses and strains that attitude and enthusiasm is number one on the list of most wanted employee characteristics.[9]

Being a "team player" is the other interpersonal non-job role in the framework. With the erosion of hierarchy and the corresponding flattening of organizational structures, teams are likely to be the main organizing work structure for the foreseeable future (Chap. 7). So being a team player is naturally another sought after attribute. Employees are increasingly participating in short- and long-term project teams; often with people they have never met, let alone worked with before. These cross-functional project teams are designed to solve problems or deal with arising issues, utilizing employees with a diversity of perspectives and a broad range of expertise. Working harmoniously and constructively with others is a priceless asset.

Being *able to work in a team* is one of the top 10 sought after employee attributes.[10] Managers recognize, understandably, that effectively cooperating with others is a prized advantage. But being a team player is not as simple as it sounds; it is a complex mix of skill, knowledge, and attitude. You need, for instance, to be:

- capable of influencing colleagues and at the same time, be open to being influenced by fellow team members;
- able to juggle the dual responsibilities of team and individual outputs;
- able to work cooperatively and harmoniously with others under duress; and
- willing and able to interact and exchange information with a variety of stakeholders.

Despite its complexity, the ability to work in team environments benefits organizations, managers and employees.

Personal Non-Job Roles

The first of the two personal non-job roles—the career development role—is concerned with the continual growth and development of the employee technically and personally. It's not an unreasonable expectation for an employee to commit to lifelong learning in their career; though we've all met people who have stopped learning and developing in their working life. When challenged, a stagnant employee often gives a lame excuse like, "I'm too old to learn anything new," or when offered a career development opportunity, they retort with, "I'm just happy doing what I have always done." Continually improving, upgrading, and expanding their skill-base and developing personally benefits not only the person, but their current and future employer in the transmuting world of work.

There are two dimensions to the career development role. One dimension relates to job-development. In essence, this involves making career decisions about education, training, and career options. The second dimension is about self-development. Self-development involves improving oneself to circuitously assist in carrying out employment responsibilities. Personal development can cover such things, for instance, as managing time and priorities more effectively, developing "people skills," and reducing stress levels. Exercising the career development role—like the other non-job roles—has benefits for the organization and the individual.

The final of the four non-job roles in the performance framework and the second of the personal non-job roles is the innovation and continuous improvement role. Whereas the career development role is about improving the individual, the innovation and continuous improvement role is concerned with improving the organization.

This role is basically about offering constructive and timely suggestions and changes in how the business can function better. Innovation and continuous improvement can cover a wide spectrum of things in the workplace. For instance, it can include:

- *improving* the quality of a product or service,
- *cutting* the time and cost of production,
- *increasing* output and safety,
- *improving* the consistency of meeting deadlines,
- *enhancing* interpersonal cooperation, or
- *streamlining* systems and processes.

For business to prosper in a VUCA environment—like the employee—the organization needs to be engaged in an endless state of growth and development; all employees can have an important role to play in this regard.

By exercising these four non-job roles, the employee's performance is extended to fulfilling their organizational role as well as their job tasks. From an organization development perspective, the non-job roles the employee performs well, not too well, or poorly impacts the performance of the enterprise. It's widely acknowledged that roles such as preserving a positive and enthusiastic attitude, exhibiting teamwork, improving one's work skills, and contributing to the betterment of the functioning of the workplace are key to organizational performance. And yet these four attributes are non-job-specific and as such, are rarely—if ever—covered sufficiently in an employee's job description. We need to incorporate them and shift to the role description.

Like specialization and QA, which we covered in the last two chapters, there's no need to completely abandon these practices, including the job description. But we need to include the non-job dimension of performance in the work document for the business and employee to reach their full potential.

In the next chapter we look at the management myth that *a business is best organized around functions*.

The Top 10 Key Points ...

1. Important non-job capabilities aren't usually taken into account during the employee selection process.
2. During the induction phase of employment, there's usually a strong emphasis on preparing the new employee to undertake their job role. There is less emphasis, however, placed on preparing the employee for their organizational role.
3. To survive and prosper in a rapidly changing marketplace, companies and employees need more than technical skills training and know-how.
4. The consequence of the belief that managers are objective decision-makers is that they avoid taking into account non-job roles in remuneration considerations.
5. The job description has insalubrious control on succession planning decisions. The choice of who replaces whom in the event of an incumbent vacating that position invariably comes down to technical mastery. Non-job performance is not factored into these decisions as much as it ought to be.

6. During the standard annual or biannual performance review interview, managers usually confine their appraisal to the technical aspects of the employee's work.
7. The first non-job role in the performance framework is the positive mental attitude and enthusiasm role.
8. The second non-job role in the performance framework is the team role.
9. The third non-job role in the performance framework is the career development role.
10. The fourth non-job role in the performance framework is the innovation and continuous improvement role.

Notes

1. Adapted from Allan, B. (2013). When an employee outgrew her job description: A case study. http://blog.thecompetencygroup.com/when-an-employee-outgrew-her-job-description-a-case-study/
2. Baker, T. (2015). *The end of the job description: Shifting from a job-focus to a performance-focus*. London: Palgrave Macmillan.
3. Ibid.
4. Bennett, N., & Lemoine, G.J. (2014). What VUCA really means for you. https://hbr.org/2014/01/what-vuca-really-means-for-you
5. Baker, T. (2015). *The end of the job description: Shifting from a Job-focus to a performance-focus*. London: Palgrave Macmillan.
6. Bruce, S. (2010). Every job has 3 descriptions. http://hrdailyadvisor.blr.com/2010/02/23/every-job-has-3-job-descriptions/
7. Baker, T. (2015). *The end of the job description: Shifting from a job-focus to a performance-focus*. London: Palgrave Macmillan.
8. Warner, J. (2012). Top 10 most valued job skills. http://blog.readytomanage.com/top-10-most-valued-job-skills/
9. Ibid.
10. Ibid.

7

Management Myth # 4—A Business is Best Organized around Functions

The newly appointed CEO, Samantha, identifies as her first major challenge, the imperative to break down the boundaries between departments in the government agency she now leads. Samantha observes the agency is organized around several "silos"—it's a typical bureaucracy. Even at the senior management level, this is evident. The most important cross-functional team— the senior management team—is disjointed and not operating as a team. Managers arrive at executive meetings with their functional "hat" on and fail to consider issues from the perspective of the overall organization. Samantha knows she has a problem and has her work cut out in breaking down these traditional departmental boundaries and the rivalries they breed.

She notices the level of cooperation between departments is negligible, even non-existent in some cases. Samantha is determined to change this. She reviews the organizational structure, based on the functional model segmented across several distinct functions.

With its concentration on vertical lines of communication, the functional model's capacity for adaptive performance is severely curtailed. Approval to make a reasonably simple decision, for instance, can pass through several hands and this can take unnecessary time.

She decides to form a number of cross-functional project teams. Samantha includes these new teams in a revised organizational chart. One team is formed to look at improving communication across the agency, for example. Representatives are chosen by the new CEO from all six departments. Another cross-functional project team is set up to review and improve several archaic systems and processes that are not consistent across the agency.

Peter, from the marketing department, is invited by Samantha to be part of one of these project teams. He is quite excited about being chosen, recognizing the need to improve cross-functional communication throughout the organization. Peter goes to talk to the marketing manager in her office. Mary is less than enthusiastic when Peter tells her about this development.

"I wish the CEO had spoken to me first," Mary said to Peter in response to the news. "I can't afford to release you to attend these 'talk fests.' Peter, you are too valuable to the department. We're already short-staffed. How often does she want you to attend these meetings?"

"I don't know," replied Peter. "She hasn't told me yet."

"Well, it sounds like a complete waste of time. Your primary responsibility is to my department, Peter," said Mary. "You're a critical person in this department, and I'll have to speak to the CEO about this and let her know my feelings."

Peter leaves Mary's office deflated and confused. He'd thought this was a great opportunity to break down the silos in the agency and improve communication across the organization. He can't understand his boss's reaction.[1]

Structuring business around specialized clusters or functions has been in existence since the birth of the bureaucracy. Taylor's scientific management philosophy was founded on the concept of workers being organized around functional specialties. Most companies still operate this way; many have tried shifting to alternative structures, such as the matrix or product models, with mixed success. It raises the question: *Is the limited success of these other organizing structures due to the models themselves, or the people who lead and work in them?*

In the matrix model, for instance, employees endeavor to keep dual lines of accountability with their hierarchical boss and their project manager. The purpose of the matrix model is to have the best of both worlds: functional control and project flexibility. Several experts argue that it's not the matrix design that's faulty; it's the people who lead them.[2] I agree.

The key to making the matrix model work—or any structural arrangement, for that matter—is two-fold: possessing and using superior interpersonal skills, and developing an entirely different attitude about the worth of the functional-based working arrangement.

The appropriate communication skills needed to make the matrix model work—or any other non-functional model—boils down to being a leader instead of behaving like a manager. It means exercising influence to get one's way, rather than using the designated authority of the managerial position in the organizational hierarchy. This is especially the case in a matrix model; the project manager doesn't have a formally titled functional position in the organizational framework. Good project managers—leading in a predominantly functional workplace—rely on their influencing capabilities before their technical prowess.

Although leadership skills are paramount, it seems counterintuitive for employees working in a fast-paced, flexible, and agile working environment to receive most of the information from one—or even two—bosses. The single vertical line of communication is the backbone of the functional-based organizing structure. Despite the deliberate efforts to move away from this archaic work arrangement, it's more challenging to escape this hierarchical power trap than it ought to be. Firms adopting a matrix design to enable the increasingly project-oriented work environment, have trouble letting go of the old hierarchy. Leaders seem powerless to prevent the vertical chain-of-command dominating decision-making over the cross-functional project work. Even with the best of intentions—with alternative organizing structures—functional thinking rules.

Changing this military mindset is the key. Before I share a new organizing model that attempts to do this, let's first understand the three most popular organizing structures and their strengths and weaknesses.

Functional Model

The *functional model* is pretty much everywhere you care to look in the world of business. Work is mostly organized around units and departments, based on common job functions. For instance, in a company with a functional structure, all marketers are grouped together in one department; all salespeople are grouped together in a separate department; and all customer service people are grouped together in a third department, and so on. The pecking order is elongated and linear in large corporations, with several layers of seniority. The functional model has very few chiefs at the top and lots of soldiers at the bottom. So the functional model centralizes decision-making; decisions are escalated up the ranks. The archetypal organizational chart reflects these characteristics. Figure 7.1 is a simple illustration of the functional model.

The four functions in the model enable specialization. Employees work together in large organizing structures with a common understanding and similar job roles and responsibilities. As the company grows, the structure is easily scalable; additional vertical layers can be added without great difficulty. Its structure is simple to comprehend, administer, alter, and illustrate. Based on the scientific management principle of specialization, its appeal is long-lasting and universal.

But the main downside of the functional model is its inherent rigidity. Barriers and conflict are commonplace, particularly between functions (departments). Cross-functional communication is stifled. Typically, managers in this structure expect their employees to obey the chain-of-command; they place greater emphasis on vertical (functional)

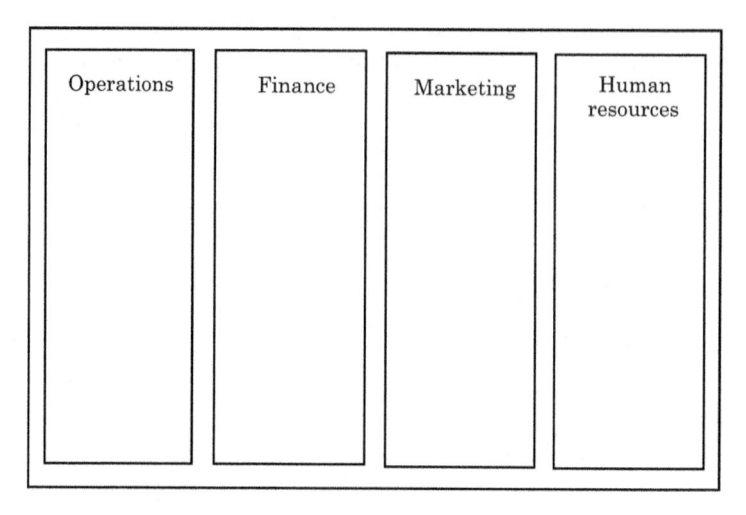

Operations	Finance	Marketing	Human resources

Fig. 7.1 Functional model

communication ahead of horizontal (cross-functional) communication. So change across the organization is slower than needed in a fast-paced marketplace. But in a stable and predictable marketplace, the functional model works fine. But it's not a suitable model for a business trying to adapt to myriad pressures and transformations in the VUCA environment we spoke of in the last chapter.

With its concentration on vertical lines of communication, the functional model's capacity for adaptive performance is severely curtailed. Approval to make a reasonably simple decision, for instance, can pass through several hands and this can take unnecessary time.

Building understanding across and between various functions of the business is problematic too. As I said, cross-functional communication isn't encouraged to the same degree as vertical communication. Ideas and collaboration are contained within silos and exposure to other functional areas—and the fresh perspective this may bring—is limited. Briefly, this structure narrows perspective and emboldens intractable rather than flexible behavior.

Matrix Model

The *matrix model*—notwithstanding its attempt to promote flexibility—is a derivative of the functional design. It's supposed to be a lithe working arrangement with negotiated task alignment between project team leaders and functional managers. In project management jargon, this is known as the "project-functional interface." Projects by their nature are horizontal because they need an assortment of skills and capabilities traversing functional boundaries. The project dimension of the matrix model attempts to redress the central weakness of the functional model.

Figure 7.2 illustrates the simple composition of the matrix model.

The four functions, as you can see in Fig. 7.2, support specialization. But overlayed on these functions is a horizontal dimension consisting of a series of projects; in this illustration there are four projects. This additional dimension supposedly improves horizontal communication channels so that the organization can perform more flexibly and responsively.

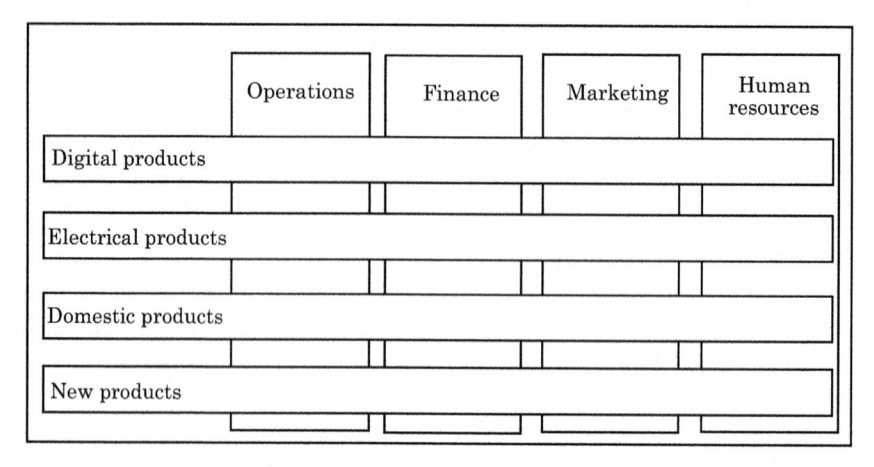

	Operations	Finance	Marketing	Human resources
Digital products				
Electrical products				
Domestic products				
New products				

Fig. 7.2 Matrix model

In practice, this isn't always smooth sailing. As Daniel Seet points out in his article, 'Power: The Functional Manager's Meat and Project Manager's Poison?':

> On paper, the dichotomy between these two entities is supportive of one another. While the project manager is concerned with what is to be done, the functional manager thinks about how the task will be done. The project manager wonders about when to do it, but the functional manager looks at where the job will be. The project manager looks at how well the whole job is completed whereas the functional manager looks at how well his own aspect has been integrated into the project. Each has different, but complementary, concerns.[3]

The reality, however, is often different. I witness frequent cases of divided loyalties, where the employee has to answer to two bosses: the project manager and their functional manager. This can degenerate into a tussle for power and territory. More often, it plays out this way: While the project manager contemplates who they can select from the functional departments to populate their team, the functional manager asks why they should release their talent, if it only benefits the project manager. The essence of the problem is that while the project manager has their own delegated authority, they don't have the same formal authority as the functional manager.

Under these conditions, functional managers flex their muscles; they've greater bargaining power over staffing arrangements. The lack of formal authority puts project managers at a disadvantage from the get-go. Matrix structures—or at least the managers involved—have failed to eliminate the dominance of the functional-based work arrangement.

Product Model

The third popular organizing structure is the *product model*. This model is predominantly structured around the business's product (or service) lines. In the product arrangement, specialists from various disciplines, instead of being scattered across a number of separate and distinct functional offices, are gathered into offices based on product line, customer type, or project. Sometimes a product team can be disbanded when its mission is accomplished, or the product becomes redundant. New product lines can also be added when appropriate; at least in theory.

Figure 7.3 illustrates a basic composition of the product model

Companies applying the matrix model still basically rely on traditional functional structures—with some adjustments to their hierarchy to sup-

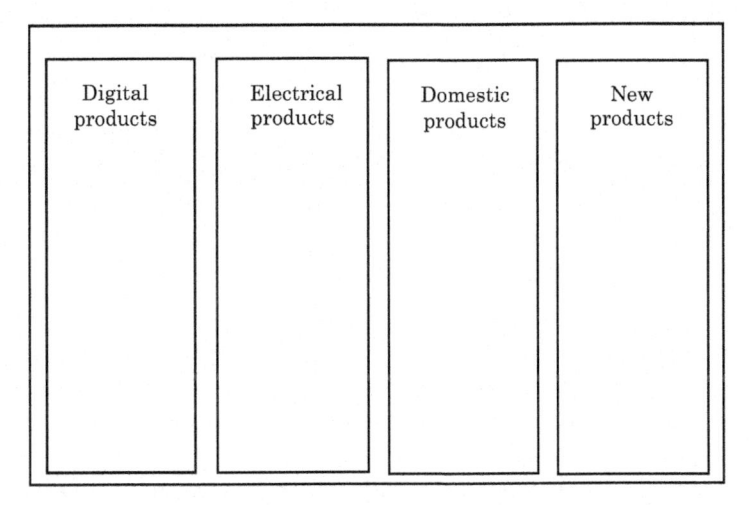

Digital products	Electrical products	Domestic products	New products

Fig. 7.3 Product model

port project teams. Product-centered organizations, on the other hand, are built around project teams as their units of production. Industries such as engineering, construction, and aerospace are examples of firms that use the product model.

There are several clear advantages in structuring organizations and people around product lines. For starters, specialists from varied disciplines now report to a common manager accountable for planning, organizing, directing, and controlling their work efforts. So the product manager is in a much better position than the functional manager to oversee the integration of the product's component parts.

In the product structure, the line-of-sight from concept to completion has greater visibility. There's a single point-of-contact for customers needing assistance. Clearer lines of accountability and responsibility have the potential to benefit the firm's customers and other stakeholders. Being multidisciplinary, this form of structure offers every employee a broader perspective of operations, opening up opportunities for the flexible deployment of the workforce (Chap. 4).

Product managers also need to be generalists; that means having a greater appreciation and understanding of the integration of all product or service operations. This model offers a good training ground for future leaders who need a grasp of the big picture. Individuals get to rub shoulders with peers from different disciplines, inevitably learning more about their colleague's work and approaches. This heightens opportunity for learning—a concept I covered in Chap. 3—an essential component of adaptability, agility, speed, and flexibility. There's far smoother and more efficient project evolution. It can be beneficial when R&D, production, engineering, logistics, field testing, maintenance, marketing and finance, and other functions collaborate early and often on the products and services the business produces or develops.

The result of this obligatory collaboration process can form the foundation for agile performance. Gains can be made in product quality, reduced cycle times, improved service, and far better positioning to recognize opportunities to capitalize on cost savings throughout the value chain. Contrast this with the functional model where "things fall through the cracks," and where it is often said, "the right hand doesn't know what the left hand is doing." Disagreements can be resolved by a manager with supervision over the entire product cycle.

Not surprisingly, quicker decisions can be made in this organizing structure than in the other two models. In comparison, with the functional structure,

- cross-functional communication channels need to be developed and consciously maintained;
- departments are forced to make compromises; and
- parallel matters such as budgeting priorities, safety procedures, and differing workloads have to be coordinated and hammered out.

All of these matters take time, unnecessary effort and duplication.

So what are the disadvantages of the product model?

There are three drawbacks with the product organizing structure. First, product offices have to compete with each other to gain essential resources from "head office," in the same way as functional silos do. This kind of resource haggling is no different to the rivalry experienced in departments lobbying for more resources from top management. Decision-making slows down and rivalries surface.

Second, a new product idea may not get proper consideration, on the basis of it not "fitting in" with an established office. The set up costs of another product line and the vested interest in not diverting resources away from the other products, renders new product development slow and challenging.

Third, the concentrated, in-depth, specialized technical capability found in functional departments isn't present in the product office. The comprehensive technical skills-set is lacking in the product model in comparison with the functional model. And ironically, pushing head office to resource additional specialists to plug specialist gaps can be more challenging than increasing the size of a department of specialists under the functional structure. An exceptional case has to be made by a product office, whereas a department can rationalize recruiting a new employee simply on the basis of being short-staffed. Resource rivalry, territorial tussles, and protection of vested interests are still familiar in businesses structured along product lines.

These three limitations of the product model can negatively affect the company's capacity to innovate and decrease processing speed—two dimensions of organizational agility.

> **Where the rubber meets the road …**
>
> **Starbucks coffee company's organizational structure**
>
> Starbucks is the largest coffee house chain in the world. The firm's industry leadership is partly attributed to its organizational structure. A company's organizational structure influences management and leadership, communication, change, and other variables critical to business success. Starbucks has evolved to have an organizational structure that matches current business needs. This structure is unique to Starbucks, although it is based on a conventional model of organizational structures. Starbucks succeeds because its organizational structure grows with the business, enabling the company to optimize processes and the quality of its goods and services.
>
> Starbucks Coffee's organizational structure changes to serve the needs of the business. This structure supports the company's goal of global expansion and diversification. Starbucks has a matrix organizational structure, which is a hybrid mixture of different features from the basic types of organizational structure. The following are the main features of Starbucks Coffee's organizational structure:
>
> *Functional structure*
>
> The functional structure of Starbucks Coffee's has an HR, finance, and marketing department. These departments are most pronounced at the top levels of the organizational structure at the corporate headquarters. For instance, the corporate HR department implements policies applicable to all Starbucks cafés. The functional feature of the firm's organizational structure facilitates top-down monitoring and control.
>
> *Geographic divisions*
>
> At present, the company has three regional divisions for the global market: China and Asia-Pacific, Americas, and Europe, Middle East, Russia and Africa. Also, in the US market, Starbucks involves further geographic divisions: Western, Northwest, South-east, and North-east. Each geographic division is overseen by a senior vice president. This way, each Starbucks manager reports to two superiors: the geographic head (e.g., the president of US operations) and the functional head (e.g., the corporate HR manager). This feature of Starbucks' structure offers closer managerial support for unique geographic needs. Each division head is given a high degree of autonomy to adjust their strategies and policies to suit specific market conditions.

(continued)

Product-based divisions
Starbucks also has product-based divisions in its organizational structure. These divisions support product lines. For example, Starbucks has a division for coffee and related products, another division for baked goods, and another division for merchandise like coffee mugs. The product-based divisions enable a focus on developing its products with support from its organizational structure.

Teams
Teams are used at the lowest organizational levels, namely, the Starbucks cafés. In each café, the firm has teams organized to deliver goods and service to customers. This feature empowers the company to provide effective and efficient service to consumers.

By 2007, the company was expanding rapidly; it subsequently shifted its focus away from customers toward strategic global expansion. However, in making this change, Starbucks experienced significant decline in sales, largely due to a lack of attention on the customer experience. When Howard Schultz resumed the CEO position in 2008, he changed Starbucks' organizational structure to emphasize the customer. New regional divisions were created, and teams at Starbucks cafés were given better training. So, the current organizational structure of Starbucks reflects this customer-focus reform and the firm's financial performance.[4]

Customer-Centric Model

Before explaining the *customer-centric model*, I should make this claim: this model of mine isn't perfect. It isn't a panacea; no organizational structure is. All organizational structures have their comparative benefits and liabilities. Each model is based on a certain set of beliefs, assumptions, and business priorities. The functional model, for instance, assumes that people of a similar skills-set will work best when grouped together. In the use of the matrix model, it is assumed that projects and functions can and should coexist in the one organizational structure. The product model is underpinned by the belief that a concentration on product lines will result in better quality goods and services. These assumptions and beliefs shape the priorities of the enterprise.

Although the product model has made a real attempt to move away from the practice of organizing work around functions, it still has structured silos that create the same problems as the functional model. So it raises the perennial questions: *What are the other organizing options? What type of structure has the potential to stimulate agile performance?*

Figure 7.4 represents a new organizing structure that attempts to minimize the liabilities of the three models we have discussed.

The first obvious characteristic of the customer-centric model is that it's structured around a series of concentric circles, as distinct from the three linear models just described. Although not unique, companies structured around circular models are rare. The vast majority of organizational structures are founded on hierarchy, with a clear top to bottom chain-of-command. Even the circular models I have cited have "top" management illustrated in the inner circle, implying a different sort of pecking order. Instead of senior management represented at the top of a linear structure, they're represented at the center of these circular models. And the rest of the organization is illustrated revolving around the "inner circle." In the circular formation, top management isn't sitting at the top

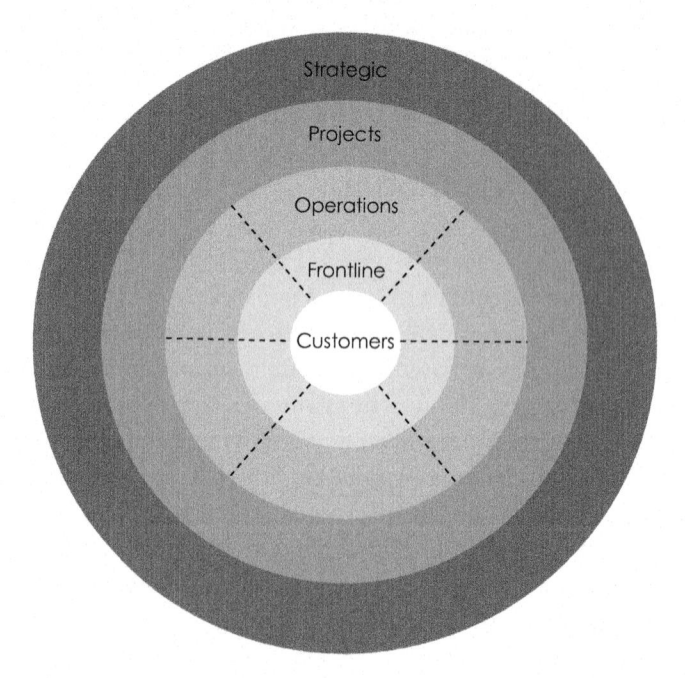

Fig. 7.4 Customer-centric model

of the pyramid sending directives down the "food chain;" they're instead at the center of the organization, spreading their vision and directives outward.[5]

So a significant difference in the model illustrated in Fig. 7.4 is that the customer is placed at the center of the organizing structure. Having the customer at the center of the organization makes a very clear statement that the end-user is fundamental to everything that happens (or doesn't happen) in the business. In simple terms, it's a model based on the concept of customer-focus, which we discussed in Chap. 5. After all, it stands to reason that the customer should have a central role, be factored into the organizing structure, and illustrated as such. This makes perfect sense if, as Peter Drucker—the prominent management thinker—once remarked succinctly, "the purpose of a business is to find and keep a customer."[6]

Another distinguishing feature of the customer-centric model is the way functions are represented. As you can see, they are depicted in this diagram with the six dotted straight lines. In the hierarchical organizing structures there's generally an absence of dotted lines. And in the matrix structures, dotted lines are generally illustrated as links to the project managers. Solid lines, as distinct from dotted lines, symbolize the functional leader having the most clout of the two bosses, despite rhetoric of equality. Dotted lines therefore show a less dominant line of reporting—or in the case of the customer-centric model—a less prominent functional boundary.

Furthermore, the dotted lines in Fig. 7.4 indicate that while there are functions, they are not the mainstay of the overall arrangement. You can see the dotted lines only extend to the *Frontline* and *Operations* strata. The cross-functional project team layer traverses departments. And the strategic layer, first and foremost, has a tactical oversight that again traverses the functions. With strategic surveillance, executive management shouldn't have the same functional fixation depicted in the scene at the beginning of this chapter. Functional-based working arrangements characteristic of both the functional and matrix models usually result in a senior manager's identity wrapped up predominantly in their departmental duties and responsibilities.

Although unlabeled, there are six functional entities shown in Fig. 7.4. Some organizations have more, or less, functional areas. The point I'm making is that while acknowledging that functional boundaries have some relevance in the structure of an organization, they shouldn't be the foremost divisions in the structure of an agile enterprise.

The executive leadership, represented in the strategic space, is primarily responsible for supporting the other layers of the business. The executive sustains the project teams, the operations, and the frontline staff so they can carry out their work to their fullest capacity. Besides, another reason the model is illustrated as a series of concentric circles is to make the point that there is no hierarchy. Everyone in the customer-centric organizing structure is on the same level, excepting of course that each stratum has a specific set of responsibilities.

If a business has clear market segments—such as overseas and domestic customers—these groups can be shown in the central circle with a series of dotted lines. The key idea though, is that the company orbits around its customers; the customer is illustrated as central in the organizational structure. Further, it reminds people working in the enterprise, that the customer is "central" to all activity in the business.

You can also see that the frontline strata, who deal directly with the customer, is segmented into several functions. This could include the production department, the administration department, and so on. Although it's quite possible an enterprise has a homogenous frontline team, absent of any functional boundaries. Either way, it's logical because of their regular interactions, that frontline employees and customers are represented together, side-by-side.

Moving out to the next strata, we have "operations." This layer of business is involved in producing the business's products or services. Product manufacturing, for example, would be part of this strata. Or, in the case of a service business, such as an engineering firm, operations include drafting. All the same, the operations strata supports the frontline with the goods and services needed to sell and service customers.

Within an operations stratum in most enterprises, there are supervisors and managers. Leaders in operations are responsible for supporting operational employees with the resources they need to perform their job role. Furthermore, with the backing of operational leaders, employees working on the frontline can properly service the needs of the business's customer-base. Leaders in the operations strata—or any other layer of the business—can be identified in this model structure.

The project team strata are illustrated beside the strategic management strata for two reasons. First, cross-functional project teams—be they permanent or temporary—are usually formed to consider changes impacting the entire organization. Therefore, these teams are strategic rather than operational in their focus. For example, a cross-functional project team can be set up to consider policies for improving the organization's culture. Due to their strategic orientation, it makes sense for cross-functional project teams to be separated from operations in the structure.

The second reason for the strategic positioning of project teams is that they are best placed to report directly to executive management. Direct access to executive management provides the necessary relevance and clout for the work of project teams. What's more, strategic teams are somewhat insulated from getting caught up in the cross-fire between functional managers and project managers—the main weakness of the matrix model. In the customer-centric model, members of project teams are also members of either an operations or frontline team. So project team participants have two bosses, similar to the matrix arrangement. But the customer-centric model makes a cleaner distinction than the matrix model between operations and projects.

An organization can have any number of project teams. Project teams can be disbanded at any time, and others instigated when necessary. For example, project teams can be formed around the following strategic matters:

- workplace culture improvement;
- rewards and incentives;
- innovation and continuous improvement;
- safety and well-being;
- recruitment and selection; and
- product and service development.

This is not an exhaustive list; it does, however, give a flavour of some areas of business that may benefit from the cross-functional perspectives of a team of employees. There are doubtlessly other areas that could benefit from the creation of a project team. The range and composition of project teams is largely dependent on the industry and the enterprise.

I favor the idea, however, of all employees—aside from their job role—participating in one project team. This may constitute an employee's organizational citizenship role. Or, putting it another way, employee involvement in project-based work can be the vehicle for performing one or more of their non-job roles—such as the team or innovation and continuous improvement roles that we covered in Chap. 6.

The final layer—the outer layer—is the strategic strata representing executive management. As I've pointed out, the executive isn't segmented into functional areas with functional responsibilities. Functional leadership—as it should—rests with leaders in the operations strata. By depicting an absence of boundaries in the strategic strata, this makes an important statement that enterprise executives should have their eye on the overall perspective of the enterprise. This is preferable to being functionally fixated.

I'll go one step further: I favor the regular rotation of executive managers. Executives ought to be flexibly deployed to oversee several, and not just one, functional area of the business. There are some advantages in this proposed system of rotation and less downside than may appear at first glance. Executive leaders, as I indicated earlier, also have responsibility for mentoring and sponsoring the work of the project teams in this model. Furthermore, their primary role is supporting the organization instead of the reverse; that is, the notion that the organization is there to support senior management! Briefly, the executive leadership's main purpose is to provide strategic direction and enable the rest of the organization to achieve that vision.

The customer-centric model is not a perfect organizing model, as I said. But it's structured to enable organizational agility. The model is an alternative framework to foster an adaptive work culture to meet the challenging external environmental demands I covered in Part I. It's a significant departure from the all too familiar formal, bureaucratic, functional structure most organizations continue to grapple with. It's also significantly different from the matrix model, with its inherent challenges with accountability and responsibility. These two models—both function-centric—are ill-equipped to promote the kind of agile performance businesses need for adaptive advantage.

Several other non-functional models have been advanced, including the product model. But as I said at the outset of this chapter, the struggle stems largely from our functional mindset rather than the structures themselves. This functional thinking stems from the long-standing indoctrination of work segmentation and specialization. We find it hard to let go of the performance management practice of functional-based work after 100 years of habit. The ideas of segmentation, specialization, and accountability all originated from the scientific approach to management. The customer-centric model is yet another opportunity to put a dint in this thinking and hopefully stimulate new ways of thinking and working in response to a VUCA marketplace.

In the next chapter, I confront the management myth that *a happy employee is a productive employee.*

The Top 10 Key Points ...

1. Structuring business around specialized clusters or functions has been in existence since the birth of bureaucracy.
2. Despite the deliberate decision of many businesses to try moving away from the functional model, it's more challenging to escape this hierarchical power trap than it ought to be.
3. The functional model is simple to comprehend, administer, alter, and illustrate.
4. The main downside of the functional model is its inherent inflexibility. Barriers and conflict are commonplace, particularly between departments.
5. The matrix model is supposed to be a lithe working arrangement with negotiated task alignment between project team leaders and functional managers.
6. But with the matrix model, there are frequent cases of divided loyalties, where the employee has to answer to two bosses: the project manager and their functional manager. It can degenerate into a tussle for power and territory.

7. In the product model, specialists from various disciplines, instead of being scattered across a number of separate and distinct functional offices, are gathered into offices based on product line, customer type, or project.
8. The limitations of the product model negatively affect the company's capacity to innovate and slows processing speed; two dimensions of agility.
9. The customer-centric model is structured on a series of concentric circles.
10. The customer-centric model is not a perfect model. But it's structured to enable organizational agility.

Notes

1. Baker, T. (2014). *Attracting and retaining talent: Becoming an employer of choice*. London: Palgrave Macmillan.
2. Seet, D. (2009). Power: The functional manager's meat and project manager's poison? https://danielseet.wordpress.com/2008/12/23/power-the-functional-manager%E2%80%99s-meat-and-project-manager%E2%80%99s-poison/
3. Ibid.
4. Meyer, P. (2015). Starbucks coffee company's organizational structure. http://panmore.com/starbucks-coffee-company-organizational-structure
5. Devaney, E. (2004). The pros and cons of 7 popular organizational structures. http://blog.hubspot.com/marketing/team-structure-diagrams
6. Jantsch, J. (2004). Fire the CEO. http://www.peace-university.net/25040.php

8

Management Myth # 5—A Satisfied Employee is a Productive Employee

Stanford University researcher Mark Lepper and his team conducted a significant research study in the early 1970s, concerned with the impact of extrinsic rewards on performance. Specifically, Lepper was interested in whether prizes influence behavior in young children.

A brand new activity was introduced to the children at a nursery. The teachers issued the children with creamy white artist's drawing paper and brand new marker pens; the children were given time to draw with these novel materials. They had never done drawings with marker pens before. Predictably, the children took to the activity with relish. But after exactly one hour, the materials were whisked away to the disappointment of the children.

Several days later, one of the researchers returned to the class and randomly divided the class into two groups to continue the new drawing activity. One group of children were taken to another room. They were given the opportunity to continue their drawings just as they had done before. After an hour, the researcher thanked the children in this group and took away the art material and their drawings.

Human spirit and work is concerned with the immersion of one's human spirit in their vocation. Sustaining an individual's spirit at work can have a positive impact in so many ways, including work performance.

The second group of children were offered a prize for drawing their pictures. It was explained to this group that some special prizes would be given to the children who drew really good pictures. The children took to their task, anticipating they might receive a prize for their picture. This control group was given the same amount of time (one hour) as the other group to compete their art work. At the end of the session, the researcher thanked the children as he'd done with the other group. But this time, he handed out a prize to each child in the control group.

One week later the researchers returned to the classroom. The afternoon period consisted of "free time;" the children could choose what they wanted to do with their time. The special paper and marker pens were placed on the tables and easily accessible for the children. However, the children had other options too. They could go outside and run around in the playground. They could play with the toys in the classroom. Or they could return to the drawing activity. The researchers observed the time the children spent on their chosen activities. To what extent would the prizes given to the children in the control group affect their choices and behavior? The researchers assumed that the children in the control group, who had received prizes, would spend more time on the drawing activity.

But that didn't happen!

The result was one the researchers didn't foresee. Their findings challenged conventional wisdom about parenting and education. The children who received the extrinsic rewards for their art work chose to spend less time drawing than those who weren't rewarded. Conversely, the children who didn't receive a prize chose to spend more of their discretionary time on the drawing activity. The children who were rewarded seemed reluctant to continue with the activity without the promise of a further reward. The initial reward paradoxically reduced the children's motivation rather than increasing it.

But what was even more surprising is this: The art work of all the children was evaluated by a group of independent judges with no knowledge of the experiment. The result was that the pictures drawn by the children who were rewarded were evaluated as less competent than the pictures drawn by the unrewarded group.

So in summary: The children who received an extrinsic reward spent less time drawing when given a choice—and when they were rewarded, they put in less effort too.[1]

Is it true that if you're satisfied with your work, you perform better? There's a widely held belief that satisfaction and performance go hand-in-hand. The pathway to better job performance—according to many managers—is through job satisfaction. This general belief has been around for at least 100 years, despite inconclusive evidence of a link between job satisfaction and job performance. This misguided conviction has led to a range of performance management measures designed to satisfy people at work. We subsequently use extrinsic rewards—usually monetary—to foster a sense of satisfaction on the job.

What is needed to increase job performance, however, is cultivating the right conditions in designing and leading work for intrinsic motivation to flourish. Engaging the "hearts and minds" of people at work is an entirely different source of motivation to being satisfied with the extrinsic rewards of one's job. We need a rethink about work motivation and the management of performance.

Admittedly, one or two studies show a causal link between job satisfaction and job performance.[2] More studies show a reverse relationship; that is, performance leads to satisfaction on the job.[3] But the clear majority of research concludes that too many other factors are in play to make the generalized claim that a satisfied employee is a higher performing employee.[4] And lots of studies show no relationship between satisfaction and performance.[5] So all the research taken together suggests we should look to other means to boost performance other than satisfying the employee with intrinsic rewards.

The answer is literally under our nose. It's work itself that has the greatest potential to improve (or reduce) personal productivity, apart from the peripheral recompenses for doing the work. Instead of only using the "carrot and stick" approach, we should concentrate on motivating people with the type of work they do and how they do it. There's no doubting a satisfied employee is better off in lots of ways in comparison with a dissatisfied employee. But we need to challenge this deeply rooted belief that extrinsic rewards bring the best out of people. Sometimes they do get results; they can be effective, now and again. But the carrot and stick isn't always effective. For widespread and sustained performance, the questions we need to ask are: *How do we engage the heart and mind of the employee in their work? How can we make the connection between human spirit and work?*

One of the main criticisms from *humanists*,[6] in their response to scientific management, is that it dehumanizes the worker. By separating the planning function from actual work accomplishment, workers needn't bother to think—the thinking has already been done by management. This division of planning and doing—as logical as it indubitably seems—strips the worker of their autonomy and self-sufficiency. Mastery of work in these circumstances is boiled down to robotically and repetitiously following a series of processes or procedures. And work broken down into small, controllable segments, is often considered meaningless by those called upon to do it, namely, workers. The humanists have a valid point.

Dave and Wendy Ulrich, in their book *The Why of Work: How Great Leaders Build Abundant Organizations That Win*, explain the significance of understanding how work contributes to a greater cause beyond simply completing a process.[7] Although I've acknowledged that the nature of work has transformed prodigiously from the days of the factory assembly line, performance management practices we use haven't kept pace. Work is still fundamentally segmented, regimented, and tightly controlled. In particular, work segmentation is still the prevailing performance management practice we discussed in Chap. 5.

Dan Pink in his popular book, *Drive: The Surprising Truth About What Motivates Us*, challenges us to think completely differently about human motivation and performance.[8] Pink tells us that the carrot and stick approach isn't always effective, especially for the relatively new breed of knowledge worker. He claims we need to do more than satisfy the employee with a sprinkling of external rewards. And I think he's right—as a growing number of authors do.

High performance doesn't stem from the promise of rewards and incentives for following a set of predetermined systems and processes. As Dan Pink puts it:

> For as long as any of us can remember, we've configured our organizations and constructed our lives around its bedrock assumption: The way to

improve performance, increase productivity, and encourage excellence is to reward the good and punish the bad.[9]

> **Where the rubber meets the road …**
>
> **Food for thought**
> Like many parents with young children, I enjoy taking my children to the circus and seeing the wonderment in their eyes from the spectacle. I take our youngest daughter to the circus every year. It's a great joy for us both. The colors, sounds, and smells; It's all an intoxicating sensory delight.
> My daughter mostly likes the show ponies. The trainer has a light whip in one hand and a pocket full of treats in the other hand. During the show, the trainer uses both the whip and treats to coax the ponies to do their impressive feats.
> It makes me think: This isn't far removed from the way we try to motivate human beings in the workplace. In fact, it is exactly the same! Human beings are treated like circus animals in the main. The manager dangles carrots in front of employees in the form of extrinsic rewards, such as bonuses, and uses sanctions to punish them when they step out of line.
> In the circus environment, reward and punishment seems to work really well to get the animals to comply. But does it work as well in the educated workplace of the twenty-first century?
> After all, reward and punishment is simple to understand, easy to monitor, and straightforward to administer.

Of course, being satisfied at work is not a bad thing; it does carry many benefits. The paybacks include having a higher than average energy level at work and being less inclined to leave and work for a competitor. So it is important for reasons such as these to cultivate a culture of satisfaction at work. But to think that job satisfaction automatically translates into better performance is a bridge too far. Job performance is complex, involving many moving parts. Some of these performance factors are characteristic of the employee themselves. Other factors have to do with the work environment. And other factors are associated with the nature of the work itself. I believe it's possible to positively influence these three factors, especially the work environment and the work itself.

Many writers, as I indicated, criticize scientific management as a dehumanizing experience. Taylor paradoxically designed his methodology in part to satisfying workers. But surely being told what to do, how to do it, and how long it should take, robs the worker of their decision-making autonomy and innate need for self-mastery. It's hard to believe that overly systemized work is stimulating to do. Nonetheless, Taylor said this about scientific management and job satisfaction:

> The task is always so regulated that the man who is well suited to his job will thrive while working at this rate during a long term of years and grow happier and more prosperous, instead of being overworked.[10]

Taylor's idea of motivation was starkly different to theories of later years. His motivational tactics started and finished with monetary incentives. According to Taylor, work "consists mainly of simple, not particularly interesting, tasks. The only way to get people to do them is to incentivize them properly and monitor them carefully."[11] But jobs have become far more multidimensional than those executed on the old assembly line. Not only have jobs become more complex, they are potentially more interesting and self-directed. Instead of trying to encouraging job satisfaction using monetary incentives—based on the misguided assumption they elevate individual performance—a review is in order. What's more, aside from the levers of reward and punishment we still persevere with, we should consider how work can ignite the human spirit. How can we organize work to be more meaningful and engaging? As an addition to using carrots and sticks to satisfy employees, there's doubtlessly plenty of scope to engage people's human spirit in the work they do.

Human Spirit and Work

The mission to find meaning in work is not a recent phenomenon. The human relation movement, originated in the 1930's Hawthorne studies,[12] was originally interested in employee happiness at work. This was a reaction to the hard edge of scientific management. In the past few decades, however, the mindboggling transformation in Western society and the rise of the knowledge worker have rekindled enthusiasm for finding meaning in work. What exactly do I mean by *human spirit and work*? How is it different from job satisfaction? And why is spirituality at work important now?

For starters, human spirit is not referring to some kind of religious conversion, or getting people to buy into a basic belief system. In essence, what it means is people partially or fully having their spiritual needs nourished through the work they do. The concept of human spirit and work refers to a sense of purpose and meaning experienced through work. It's basically about gaining—not losing—a sense of self-esteem from work. This self-worth goes beyond being satisfied and enjoying the extrinsic rewards received in exchange for a high standard of performance. Human spirit and work is concerned with the immersion of one's human spirit in their vocation. Sustaining an individual's spirit at work can have a positive impact in so many ways, including work performance.

I think there are several reasons for the growing appetite of finding purpose and meaning from work. First, the employee now—more than ever before in history—feels alienated from their workplace. Relentless organizational restructuring and downsizing, reengineering, and layoffs; commonplace in the past few decades, demoralize employees—mainly those who lose their job! Throw into the mix the growing inequality of wages, and rising disengagement that shows up in numerous engagement survey results around the world. People yearn for a more humanizing workplace.

Second, isn't it ironic that we've never been more connected digitally and yet—at a human level—we have never been so disconnected? We can, at a click of a button, connect with someone in the far flung regions of the world in seconds. This digital connectivity and the wonderful benefits it brings is a relatively recent phenomenon. But inversely, there's been a rapid decline in human connectivity within our communities. We don't know our neighbors, let alone who lives across the road. We have no idea who services our car, let alone who serves us at the corner store. Yet, human beings have a deep hunger for human connection, which is deeper than "connecting" with friends on Facebook. So the workplace can—and does, to a certain extent—fill this void.

Today's workplace—despite our feelings of emotional isolation—is a principle source of community. The decline in Western society of neighborhoods, churches, civic groups, and extended families as the traditional sources of emotional attachment are being somewhat replaced by the workplace community. For many people, the workplace provides the only consistent link to other people and to the human needs of connection and contribution.

Third, our digital connectivity doubtlessly brings with it lots of wonderful benefits. We become exposed to more ideas, philosophies, and perspectives than ever before in history. Eastern philosophies are no longer as mysterious to Westerners. Eastern philosophies have encouraged Westerners to look at alternative forms of spirituality. There is growing curiosity in Buddhism and Confucianism, for instance. Zen Buddhism and Confucianism encourage practices such as meditation and emphasize values of loyalty to one's group. This way of thinking is really about discovering one's spiritual center in any activity. Ideas such as these are finding greater acceptance and application in Western society. These time-honored beliefs are shaping the way we think about our lives and the meaning of the work we do.

With a large slice of the workforce contemplating retirement and about to depart the workforce, *baby boomers* are reflecting on their legacy and the meaning of their lives. As aging baby boomers move closer to life's greatest certainty—death—they naturally have a growing interest in contemplating life's meaning. I know I do! This reflection brings with it a concentration on the contributions people make (or don't make) in their working lives.

Fourth, escalating global competition has, in the past two decades, shifted attention from machines to people as the primary source of competitive edge. Technological tools are now a commodity, easily accessible, and no longer the differentiator between competing enterprises they once were. High-performing people are in great demand worldwide and across all industries. The relentless pressure of global competition has escalated the value of people's creative energy; thinking outside the box is the new paradigm. Harnessing and maximizing people's ideas and creativity involves the collaboration of head and heart; innovative thinking is a rich source of adaptive advantage.

Yet as "new capitalism" changes the conditions of work, the individuals' connection to the organization is more tenuous. The acceleration of change and mounting uncertainty is turning work and the workplace into a place of considerable insecurity. Where work was once a stable and predictable pillar in one's life, today people are changing jobs as fast as they can surf the net for new opportunities. Job security is a romantic memory of a bygone age.

People want and need more from work than just a job. But instead, people are told there is "no long-term." The widening gulf between turmoil in the marketplace and the growing need for what famous psychologist Abraham Maslow describes as *self-actualization*, is causing great stress in workplaces everywhere. On the one hand, the trends in Western society for the humanization of the workplace heighten the hunger for meaningful working environments. But on the other hand, marketplace volatility makes it ever more challenging for employees and employers to respectively seek and provide meaningful work. Perhaps this extending gulf may partially explain the continual practice of using extrinsic motivational tools to keep the employee satisfied?

Extrinsic rewards are nevertheless less effective than previously thought. And there's no doubting that people want more from their work than the promise of bonuses. There are opportunities to bridge this widening gap. Work promises more than a source of income; it's potentially a vehicle for fostering personal growth, well-being, and purpose for greater numbers of people.

When external rewards are used, like bonuses, to fuel better performance, it ironically takes the employee's attention off the work the reward is designed to improve. How can this be? The promise of a bonus shifts the employee's focus from the task to the prize. In other words, the work becomes the means to the end result: a reward. Refer back to the research at the beginning of this chapter; extrinsic rewards can reduce, not increase performance. With the bonus top-of-mind, it's unsurprisingly common for employees to cut corners, do whatever it takes, or even cheat to get their hands on the prize. As well intended as they are—and as effective as they can sometimes be—extrinsic rewards can back-fire and be counterproductive too.

The idea of using monetary incentives to induce greater performance is deeply rooted in our psyche. Workers were once viewed as a vital cog in the factory machine. Bonus pay was issued to workers who performed the right work, the right way, within the right timeframe. Worker conformity was part of the machinery of the factory. The carrot and the stick were the levers to reinforce orthodoxy. Today, we perpetuate this approach; we try to motivate employees with a suite of rewards and the occasional sanction. Little has changed in the way we kindle performance, even though the work we do is entirely different.

The underlying belief is that the best—some would say, the only—way to enforce performance is to reward and punish work behaviors (or lack of behaviors). But if a job's only real purpose is to receive a wage and the occasional bonus without any real sense of freedom and self-sufficiency, or opportunities to grow and develop, work can't promote the employee's well-being past *paying the bills*. Though an employee may feel satisfied with this arrangement, it's hardly likely to lead to inspired work performance. We need a new game plan.

So what's the solution to this worn-out performance management practice of using extrinsic sources of motivation to enhance employee performance?

Dan Pink makes a compelling argument for using intrinsic rather than extrinsic motivation strategies to tap people's human spirit. Pink says it is time to move past the carrot and stick. True motivation he claims, comes from our intrinsic or internal belief in what we do. Instead of attempting to control work productivity with extrinsic rewards and sanctions, the work itself is the often an untapped source of self-motivation. But how can people find stimulation in their job when a large portion of what we do at work is drudgery?

Pink claims the three drivers of human endeavor are *autonomy*, *mastery*, and *purpose*. Superior performance is a natural consequence of these three innate human tendencies. These internal human drivers, when present in any activity—work-related or otherwise—tap into our human spirit. Work that has the opportunity to exercise these intrinsic motivational forces connects the human spirit with work.

Let's look at autonomy, mastery, and purpose and some practical implications for enhancing performance. Briefly, autonomy is our desire to be self-directed. Mastery is our urge to get better and better at what we do. And purpose is our thirst to be part of something larger than ourselves. This is the essence of intrinsic motivation.

Autonomy

Autonomy means being the master of our own destiny. Human beings in most cases have an instinctive need to make their own decisions, choose their priorities, do things in their own way, and develop their own approaches. The way work is organized, however, flies in the face of this natural human inclination. Performance management practices are mostly about directing, controlling, monitoring, evaluating, and planning the work employees do.

People want to be led, but they don't want to be controlled. Self-direction means having choices, options, and a certain amount of freedom to decide on courses-of-action. Without doubt, there's considerably more latitude than is currently the norm to give employees greater autonomy to decide what needs to be done, when it needs to be done, and how it can be done.

More specifically, the intrinsic driver for autonomy can be expressed in four ways in the workplace. Dan Pink refers to this as the four T's around autonomy: There is the *task, time, technique,* and *team*.[13] The "task" refers to the freedom to decide the priorities of one's work. "Time" is the decision on how much time to take to complete a task; in other words, setting deadlines. The "technique" means the freedom to decide how a task ought to be done. And "team" is deciding who to work with to complete the task or activity. It's a simple, comprehensive model that serves as a useful framework for expressing autonomy in the workplace.

Here's how it can be applied. You'll recall in the previous chapter, I recommended that every employee be given the opportunity to serve in a cross-functional project team. That project team would work on a strategic challenge or opportunity facing the organization. Why not allow the employee a percentage of their employment time to work in these teams and on projects? Set some ground rules for project-based work. Some of these ground rules might include:

- A timeframe for producing something useful or tangible.
- Access to a designated executive manager as a mentor.
- Freedom to decide what project the team member would like to work on and how they go about it.
- Some freedom to meet off-site and virtually.

I've worked with many such teams and I am always pleasantly surprised by what they come up with, and the collective energy in the project work. Autonomy to *work on the business rather than in the business* satisfies this need for self-direction, and ultimately supports the business too. Apart from a few common sense *rules*, the project teams should have complete autonomy as to how they arrive at their *solution*.

This means the project team is *free* to choose how they go about their work (task); *free* on what they spend their time on to get the project done (time); *choose* how they accomplish their work (technique); and *choose* who they involve in the project beyond their project team members (team).

Mastery

Mastery refers to the desire to get better and better. Our workplaces have a checklist mentality; they are places with too much compliance and too little engagement. As Pink eloquently puts it, compliance "might get you through the day, but only (engagement) will get you through the night."[14] Organizations benefit by fully supporting the development their employee's capabilities. We discussed the concept of flexible deployment in Chap. 4 and a tool for coordinating this: the skills matrix.

The driver for flexibly deploying an employee's skills is transitioning away from specialization and its shortcomings. Yet another driver for flexible deployment is mastery across a wider array of competencies outside the employee's job specification. Apart from tapping intrinsic motivational forces, flexible deployment—as mentioned in Chap. 3—assists the employability of the person and cultivates a climate of agility for the business.

So, as well as employability, a coordinated flexible deployment program offers more opportunities for mastery in a wider variety of tasks and skills. You'll recall I suggested using extrinsic rewards, in the form of bonus pay, for the successful mastery of new skills. This might sound contradictory. But the idea of these bonuses is to make a clear statement that flexible deployment—as opposed to specialization—is an important building block for agile performance. But the inherent internal drive for mastery ought to be the primary motivation from the person's perspective.

I've more to say about development and mastery in Chap. 10.

Purpose

Purpose is the pursuit of something bigger than ourselves; it's a cause; a driving force. As Pink rightly says, "The most deeply motivated people—not to mention those who are more productive and satisfied—hitch their desires to a cause larger then themselves."[15] Renowned management guru Gary Hamel challenges management to consider human spirit as a motivational force:

> The goals of management are usually described in words like 'efficiency,' 'advantage,' 'value,' 'superiority,' 'focus,' and 'differentiation.' Important as these objectives are, they lack the power to rouse human hearts.[16]

Business leaders, he goes on to say, "must find ways to infuse mundane business activities with deeper, soul-stirring ideals, such as honor, truth, love, justice, and beauty. Humanize what people say and you may well humanize what they do."[17] It's in our DNA to seek purpose. This is what Dave and Wendy Ulrich refer to as the *why* of work and what Simon Sinek covers in his popular book: *Start with Why*.[18]

This means leaders explaining the overriding purpose of the tasks, projects, and activities employees are involved in. In practice, when asking someone to complete any type of work—regardless of how routine or trivial it is—the manager should explain the consequences of doing (and not doing) the job well. Managers shouldn't make the mistake of assuming all employees understand the implications of the work they do; they often don't.

Let me illustrate the point with a simple example. Even a mundane task, such as sweeping the floor in the production area of a business, can be put into a positive context. The production supervisor points out to the seemingly blasé sweeper that the company is hosting an important potential customer after the shift. The company wants to make the very best impression on this important visitor. If the right impression is made—which includes the tidiness on the production floor—it may result in this customer being persuaded to place a significant order of product worth hundreds of thousands of dollars. Everyone has a role to play in winning this customer's business, including the person asked to sweep the floor of the production area. This explanation provides context to what otherwise would appear an insignificant job; that employee then understands the higher purpose than just sweeping the floor.

Imagine for a moment the difference it could make if all business leaders—for every task, big and small—explained the *why*; what a difference it would make in fostering a higher level of intrinsic employee motivation.

Communicating purpose can be done in a variety of ways. It can involve sharing some positive customer feedback; illustrating how the end-user benefits from the work employees do for them. We don't consider communicating purpose enough for two main reasons: the extra time it takes and the assumption that the employee already "gets it." Granted, employees in certain industries, such as the not-for-profit sector, have an easier time appreciating the connection between their work and the tangible results of that work in the community. But with a little thought, an appreciation of its effectiveness, and taking the time to explain the overriding purpose, leaders can make a significant contribution to motivation. This creates the right environment for the employee's human spirit to be ignited, by explaining the higher purpose of their work.

This brings us to the end of the chapter. Satisfying employees with extrinsic rewards for the work they do is important, but only part of the picture. Better performance comes doubtlessly from involving people in the work itself. There is a widely held management myth that the carrot and stick is the only effective way to stimulate work performance. Striving to capture human spirit in people's work is often neglected on the grounds it can't be achieved. Yet it's a powerful and viable motivator. We've covered three ways of doing this: Give people more freedom and the autonomy to make their own decisions about the work they do; provide them with opportunities to grow and develop; and explain the purpose of work. As Pink reminds us, "we have a deep-seated desire to direct our own lives, to extend and expand our abilities, and live a life of purpose."[19]

In the next chapter, I want to challenge the belief that *a loyal employee is an asset to the business.*

The Top 10 Key Points …

1. There is a widely held belief that satisfaction and performance go hand-in-hand despite the inclusive research about this link.
2. Instead of only using the carrot and stick approach to motivate employees, we should concentrate on motivating people with the work tasks they do and how they are executed.
3. In the past few decades, the mindboggling transformation in Western society and the rise of the knowledge worker have rekindled enthusiasm for finding meaning in work.
4. The concept of human spirit and work refers to a sense of purpose and meaning experienced through work.
5. Extrinsic rewards are less effective than we previously thought. And there is no doubting that people want more from their work than the promise of bonuses. The idea of using monetary incentives to induce greater performance is deeply rooted in our psyche.
6. Instead of attempting to control work productivity with extrinsic rewards and sanctions, the work itself is the often untapped source for self-motivation.
7. The three drivers of human endeavor are autonomy, mastery, and purpose.
8. Autonomy is our desire to be self-directed.
9. Mastery is our urge to get better and better at what we do.
10. Purpose is our thirst to be part of something larger then ourselves.

Notes

1. Yeung, R. (2011). *I is for Influence: The new science of persuasion*. London: Macmillan.
2. Keaveney, S.M., & Nelson, J.E. (1993). Coping with organizational role stress: Intrinsic motivational orientation, perceived role benefits, and psychological withdrawal. *Journal of the Academy of Marketing Science*, 21, 113–124.
   Shore, L.M., & Martin, H.J. (1989). Job satisfaction and organizational commitment in relation to work performance and turnover intentions. *Human Relations*, 42, 625–638.

3. Brown, S.P., Cron, W.L., & Leigh, T.W. (1993). Do feelings of success mediate sales performance-work attitude relationships? *Journal of the Academy of Marketing Science*, 21, 91–99.

   Darden, W.R., Hampton, R., & Howell, R.D. (1989). Career versus organizational commitment: Antecedents and consequences of retail salespeople's commitment. *Journal of Retailing*, 65, 80–105.

   MacKenzie, S.B., Podsakoff, P.M., & Ahearne, M. (1998). Some possible antecedents of in-role and extra-role salesperson performance. *Journal of Marketing*, 62, 87–98.

4. Judge, T.A., Bono, J.E., Thoresen, C.J., & Patton, G.K. (2001). The job satisfaction-job performance relationship: A qualitative and quantitative review. *Psychological Bulletin*, 127 (3), 376–407.
5. Ibid.
6. *Humanism* is a philosophical and ethical stance that emphasizes the value and agency of human beings, individually and collectively.
7. Ulrich, D., & Ulrich, W. (2010). *The why of work: How great leaders build abundant organizations that win.* New York: McGraw-Hill.
8. Pink, D.H. (2009). *Drive: The surprising truth about what motivates us.* New York: Riverhead Books.
9. Ibid.
10. Taylor, F.A. (1919). *The principles of scientific management.* New York: Harper & Brothers.
11. Pink, D.H. (2009). *Drive: The surprising truth about what motivates us.* New York: Riverhead Books.
12. https://en.wikipedia.org/wiki/Human_relations_movement
13. Pink, D.H. (2009). *Drive: The surprising truth about what motivates us.* New York: Riverhead Books.
14. Ibid.
15. Ibid.
16. Hamel, G. (2009). Moon shots for management. *Harvard Business Review*, 87, 91–98.
17. Ibid.
18. Sinek, S. (2009). *Start with why.* New York: Penguin.
19. Pink, D.H. (2009). *Drive: The surprising truth about what motivates us.* New York: Riverhead Books.

9

Management Myth # 6—A Loyal Employee is an Asset to the Business

"These three employees have demonstrated outstanding loyalty to our company," claimed Jim. "They've been working here for 25 years. I think we should reward them at the Christmas party."

"What did you have in mind, Jim?" asked Chris, Jim's boss.

"I thought we should buy them each a flat-screen plasma TV and present it to them at the Christmas party. What do you think?" said Jim with enthusiasm.

Chris looked at Jim pensively and paused. "What signal will this send the troops, Jim?" "It'll send a signal to staff that we value them; we care about them. It demonstrates that we value loyalty in our staff," Jim replied with a confident tone in his voice.

There was a longer pause and Chris asked, "What about commitment? Does it show that we value commitment?" "What do you mean, Chris? Aren't they the same thing—loyalty and commitment?" Jim asked, with a puzzled look on his face.

What the agile enterprise needs is a committed employee more than a loyal one.

"No, I don't think so. You can be loyal without being committed and committed without being loyal," Chris replied. "What do you mean?" came Chris's response.

"You have a university degree, don't you, Jim?" "Yes, I do," Jim replied. "Well, you must have shown a certain level of commitment to complete that qualification, right? But that doesn't necessarily mean you remain loyal to the university that issued you your qualification, does it?" "I guess not," said Jim.

"Similarly, a university student can be loyal to a partner in a short-term relationship, but that doesn't necessarily mean there is a long-term commitment for life," Chris continued.

"Remember this, Jim, the only rats that leave a sinking ship are the ones that can swim. Sometimes we don't want or need people to stay with the company for a long time. It's what people do that's important, not how long people decide to stay."

After another long pause, Jim posed the question, "Should we be rewarding loyalty or commitment?"

"I'm not against recognizing these three employees for their length of service. But I think we should balance this by recognizing those employees who are committed to assisting our company achieve its business goals," Chris replied.

"Okay, I get your point. I'll rethink this and get back to you," Jim said, like he'd been hit across the back of the head with a lump of wood.[1]

Many business leaders still believe that loyal employees are one of the keys to business success. After all, loyal employees stay with their current employer longer, while others move on, looking for greener pastures. This interpretation of loyalty—the willingness to remain with their current employer—is commonly considered a positive. The argument goes something like this: A long-serving employee contributes to performance over the long term, steadies the ship in turbulent times, reduces turnover and the costs associated with that, and so on. These loyal workers invest a greater portion of their career with one, or a few, companies.

But a loyal employee isn't always a high performer. An employee loyal to a company is generally bound to the systems and processes used in the organization. But they may not always "see the forest for the trees." Often a loyal employee is intent on pleasing their boss, not "rocking the boat." They can be reluctant to embrace and support new ideas.

What the agile enterprise needs more than a loyal employee, is a committed employee. A committed employee may be a short-term prospect; they may decide to leave sooner than a loyal employee. But while they're employed, they're committed to helping the business achieve its goals. What about both; a loyal and committed worker? Isn't that the ultimate answer to high performance?

Although this sounds perfect, a loyal and committed employee think differently. A loyal employee values the *status quo*; they like things the way they are; they don't like change. Whereas, a committed employee welcomes change; they are more inclined to look for new ways of doing things, faster, better and quicker; they are open to new ideas, if they believe it'll improve things. So given a choice—with all other factors equal—the committed employee is more suited to the agile enterprise.

I should also point out that being organizationally committed is not necessarily the same as having one's human spirit tied to work (Chap. 8). To be clear: Human spirit describes the emotional connection to the work, while having a sense of commitment is based on the organization's purpose. It's of course quite possible to have an attachment to both the work and the organization.

To illustrate: Jackie's work as a nurse is very stimulating and meaningful; she finds nursing, and particular her interactions with patients, engaging. Her human spirit is nurtured by the work she does. But she feels no sense of commitment to her employer—the private hospital she works for. Jackie thinks the hospital is more interested in making money than saving lives. She has difficult working relationships with most of the hierarchy. Jackie doesn't feel any obligation to the hospital because of this.

This idea can work in reverse too. Consider Kane. Kane is an apprentice chef in a large and busy restaurant. He doesn't find his work the least bit stimulating. Being a junior chef, Kane is left with the jobs no one else wants to do; for example, washing the dishes or sweeping the kitchen floor. But he loves his boss who is tolerant, kind, and understanding; for example, Kane's boss is very accommodating with his need to take care of his elderly mother, who is incapacitated. Also, Kane has the opportunity to learn his trade in the presence of some very successful chefs. Kane feels obligated to the business, even though he finds his work meaningless.

The loyal employee of the twentieth century received a comfortable salary and retirement plan in exchange for remaining with an employer for their entire working life—or at least a sizable chunk of it. The productivity of loyal employees varied, as it still does. But the key point is that *loyalty* and *performance* weren't—and aren't—inexorably linked. Taylor believed the remedy for the non-productive worker was the systemization and management of work to guarantee at least a minimum acceptable workload, carried out in a set way. He didn't believe the path to productivity was about seeking out the extraordinarily committed worker. Loyalty was the prevailing value.

Gary Hamel in his article, *Three Forces Disrupting Management*, explains the evolution of loyalty:

> This transition from an agrarian and craft-based society to an industrial economy required an epical re-socialization of the workforce. Unruly and independent-minded farmers, artisans and day laborers had to be transformed into rule-following, forelock-tugging employees. And 100 years on, this work continues, with organizations around the world still working hard to strap rancorous and free-thinking human beings into the straitjacket of institutionalized obedience, conformance, and discipline.[2]

It's hardly surprising then that this management myth—that a loyal employee is an asset to the business—is still in practice today.

Displaying loyalty to an employer is not what it used to be, and understandably so. The employee of today needs to constantly upgrade and renew their skills-set to maintain their employability. To keep current, the employee needs to take charge of their own career; leaving their career in the hands of their employer is no longer—if it ever was—a wise move. Relying upon their employer to sponsor the career development of an employee is dangerously misguided.

As I've pointed out, commitment is now a more realistic value than loyalty. The employer has an opportunity to strengthen—or weaken—this sense of commitment to the company. Business leaders can implement several practical strategies to generate more commitment from employees to the organization and its mission. These approaches consciously align employee career aspirations with the company's goals, wherever this may be feasible. We'll cover some specific strategies shortly.

However, most business leaders still overrate employee loyalty, despite the fact that it's misguided to do so. The lifetime contract between individual and organization expired more than 30 years ago. People today rightly are more inclined to display loyalty to their careers ahead of their current employer. Employees aren't planning to work for decades for one company. Not only are employees not expecting to work for a single employee their whole career, they don't want to either. What's more, most employees are disillusioned with the idea of displaying blind loyalty to their employer.

But, at the same time, people don't like the idea of changing jobs and shifting from business-to-business every six months, for their entire working life. It's not attractive for companies either; they would grind to a halt if they had to replace large portions of the workforce every six months. So if long-term loyalty is dead and buried, how can organizations and employees happily coexist in turbulent times?

Is there an avenue for employees and employers to strike a new working agreement; one that isn't based on long-term loyalty? This arrangement would be one that offers businesses the focus and expertise needed to compete in the marketplace, on the one hand. And on the other hand, it would be an arrangement that provides employees with attractive career benefits they need to survive and prosper. The answer is *yes*—a new working arrangement can be struck—but only if companies let go of this misguided belief that a loyal worker is a good worker.

Obviously businesses need a committed and competent workforce. And the employee needs the opportunity to remain employable. A new contract—a new psychological contract—can be achieved for mutual benefit around these needs.[3] This new psychological contract promises to be a very appealing exchange, particularly when the skills a person masters further their career and are the capabilities that are also required by the company that sponsor them.

But we must let go of the notion of sentimental loyalty. The new psychological contract is supported by commitment, not loyalty. Commitment is a more pragmatic exchange than loyalty. A person can be committed to something or someone without necessarily displaying long-term, sentimental loyalty. As I mentioned earlier, in the opening scene of this chapter, a graduating student requires a certain amount of commitment to completing their university degree, without necessarily being loyal to the institution conferring the degree. Similarly, a person can display a sense of loyalty, without being committed.

For example, someone can be faithful and devoted to a person without committing to a particular course-of-action. A person may claim loyalty to someone, but can at times break their promises to them, in other words. This of course occurs frequently in all walks of life. It therefore follows that feeling a sense of loyalty doesn't always translate into a dogged commitment to perform at a high level. Equally, if an employee demonstrates commitment to achieving the goals of the business, it doesn't always follow that they are bindingly loyal to the enterprise. Given a choice between loyalty and commitment, business leaders should opt for commitment every time.

At the same time, it's in the best interests of the employee to seek commitment from their employer to support them to achieve their personal objectives. The mistaken assumption is that loyalty means *forever*. But even when a company loses a star performer to a competitor, it doesn't mean the departing employee wasn't committed in the short term; they probably were; that's why they are considered *talent*. As a university student expressed it to me recently,

> It's like dating: You can be faithful to the person you're seeing now while you're involved with them, but that doesn't mean you won't move on and date someone else later.

A company shouldn't—and increasingly cannot—strive to keep all their top talent forever; as appealing as that might sound. So instead of loyalty, modern corporations ought to cultivate mutual commitment between employer and employee, albeit, on a shortened timeframe.

I therefore define commitment as the employee's psychological attachment to the organization, as distinct from the work they are employed to perform. However, there is conceivably some cross-over with job satisfaction and organizational identity; that is, the degree to which an employee experiences a sense of oneness with their company. Although they are all different concepts, there is some relationship between commitment, satisfaction, and identification. Organizational scientists have developed many definitions of organizational commitment, and numerous scales to measure it.

One of the most notable models of commitment is John Meyer and Natalie Allen's; their model was developed to bring together the various definitions of commitment.[4] According to Meyer and Allen, there are three thought processes that characterize an employee's commitment to an organization. These dimensions are labeled as *affective, continuance,* and *normative* commitment. Let's briefly consider each and then look at what an enterprise can do to improve (or reduce) an employee's commitment.

The Desire to Stay

Affective commitment is the employee's emotional attachment to the organization. An employee with strong affective commitment identifies with the purpose of the business and has a desire to remain a part of the firm because they believe in the products or services it delivers. Commitment in this light is characterized as wanting to stay and be part of this mission. The desire to stay is based on a belief in what the business is setting out to achieve. This cause, for example, could be a not-for-profit organization that feeds the homeless. There is a desire to commit to what the organization does and a willingness to assist in helping the organization fulfill its mission.

The Cost of Leaving

Continuance commitment is defined as the employee's attachment to the organization because of the costs of leaving to work somewhere else. The individual commits to the organization on the basis that they perceive a high personal cost in leaving to work elsewhere. This loss could be financial, such as losing superannuation accruals. It could also be a social cost in moving away from friends and work colleagues. So the employee stays put and commits because they feel they have to, in the belief they would be worse off leaving to work somewhere else.

The Feeling of Obligation

Normative commitment is defined as the employee's attachment out of a sense of obligation. The individual commits to and remains with a company because of a feeling of indebtedness. When a company helps the employee acquire a new set of skills that supports their professional and personal advancement, for instance, the employee may feel a sense of obligation. In reciprocation, the employee is prepared to assist the business achieve its objectives.

There is an interesting paradox when an organization helps an employee to build their skills-set in exchange for their commitment. By helping an employee develop themselves beyond the scope of their current job—instead of leaving and finding a better job matching this new skills-set—the employee can sometimes feel an obligation to stay with their current employer. The employee's sense of commitment to their current employer is based on the intrinsic motivation that comes from the concept of mastery we talked about in the last chapter.

For instance, the company may have invested resources in training an employee; this person feels grateful and returns the favor by increasing their performance on the job and remaining employed with the company to "repay the debt." A feeling of obligation can also reflect an internalized norm, developed before the person joins the company, through family or other forms of socialization that one should display a sense of loyalty to their employer. Put simply, the employee stays with the organization because they "ought to."

To summarize, Meyer and Allen's model characterizes organizational commitment in three ways: a desire to stay, the cost of leaving, and a sense obligation to the employer. Employees with strong affective commitment stay because they want to; those with strong continuance commitment stay because they have to; and those with strong normative commitment stay because they feel they ought to.

Commitment, whichever way, is a joint venture between employer and employee. The implications for enterprises wanting to promote these three dimensions are fairly obvious. If the enterprise can communicate an inspiring and compelling purpose, it has the potential to instill a desire to commit from employees. If the organization can make it hard to leave, by providing financial and social incentives, employees may think twice about leaving and stay committed to their current employer. And finally, by helping to support employees both personally and professionally, with such inducements as flexible working arrangements to manage work and home responsibilities, employees may feel a reciprocal sense of obligation to their employer. So in brief, painting a compelling vision, offering inducements to stay, and investing resources to grow and develop all help inculcate a value of commitment.

Employee commitment can waver. Commitment levels fluctuate more dramatically than a sense of loyalty, which can remain relatively constant. What's more, the three dimensions of commitment affect people in different ways. A person can be committed in an affective, normative, and continuance sense, in varying levels of intensity.

The commitment profile of each person can be an assortment of high, low, and medium levels in the three dimensions, at any one time. Furthermore, the employee's commitment profile affects their workplace behavior in many different ways. It will influence job and non-job performance, levels of absenteeism, and the prospects of leaving for another job opportunity in varying degrees of intensity.

How does employee commitment affect performance? John Meyer's research indicates that employees who want to stay because they believe in the good work of the organization (affective commitment), tend to perform at a higher level than those who don't. Employees who remain out of a sense of obligation (normative commitment) also tend to outperform those who feel no such obligation, but the effect on performance is not as strong as that observed in employees who have a desire to stay (affective commitment). Employees who feel they have to stay primarily to avoid losing something of value (continuance commitment), such as a bonus or losing seniority, often have little incentive to do anything more than is required to retain their position.[5] So, not all forms of commitment result in high performance.

Let's consider some practical things that can be done to enhance commitment and performance.

Aligning Career Growth with Company Goals

An effective way of positively impacting more than one dimension of commitment is aligning career development with company goals. How can this be accomplished? When an enterprise assists a person in developing their expertise to further their professional and personal growth and development, it can build commitment. Under these circumstances, research suggests the employee generally feels a sense of obligation to support the organization to achieve its goals.[6] If the learning opportunity is ongoing, the employee may also experience continuance commitment. In other words, the employee considers it a prohibitive cost to personally foot the bill for the remainder of the course. So they decide not to leave to work somewhere else before completing the program. As a result, a relevant organizationally-sponsored development program that supports career and company goals can assist in increasing an employee's continuance and normative commitment levels.

How does a business leader confirm alignment between what the employee wants and what the company needs? The starting point is an open discussion between the manager and employee about their career aspirations. It's also helpful to discuss any connection between the employee's professional and personal goals and the company's strategic direction. When people understand the larger picture, they can readily see how to advance (or not advance) their own careers with their current employer.

It should also be acknowledged that frank and frequent dialogue about careers can decrease—rather than increase—employee commitment. An employee with great promise may part ways with their current employer when they discover they can't achieve their career aspirations where they are. But on balance, honest and regular dialogue between leaders and team members is more likely to benefit both the individual and organization.

More and more companies are seeing the benefits of using assessment tools and career coaches to identify employees' strengths and decide how best to leverage those talents in their current job role. An increasing number of companies are also encouraging employees to discuss with their boss how their strengths and talents can be best used in their current and future positions within the business. I think this is a very positive move. When employees use more of their innate talents, they find their work more satisfying, and may well feel a greater sense of commitment to their current place of work.

Harriet is an accountant. The company she works for uses assessment tools and career coaching. When she expressed interest in a management position, her career coach reminded Harriet that her assessment indicated strengths in areas other than management. Harriet then admitted that her interest in management stemmed primarily from the managerial position's earning potential. She couldn't see any other way to increase her earning capacity beyond leaving to work somewhere else. Based on Harriet's interest and commitment to furthering her career, the company offered her the position of revenue analyst. Based on Harriet's educational background and strengths—including attention to detail and adherence to company policies and procedures—the position of revenue analyst was a logical fit. In this new role, she provided more value to the company and took on new challenges. Harriet also increased her earnings because the new position rated several grades higher than her former position as an accountant. So career and company alignment makes sense and can positively affect all three forms of commitment we've discussed.

Design Work with Variety and Autonomy

We've already discussed the significance of variety (Chap. 4) and autonomy (Chap. 8) in work design. A job that offers variety and the freedom to make significant decisions and minor mistakes in a safe environment can engender commitment from the incumbent. Allowing staff to take ownership of projects gives them the opportunity to develop new skills and, just as importantly, the chance to demonstrate what they are capable of.

Designing work with some variability and scope for freedom takes thought and planning. It is, nevertheless, worth the effort. But at the very least, the manager ought to let employees know how and when they can exercise choices in their work role. As a simple and practical illustration, a public relations firm I consult to uses their weekly staff meeting to share responsibility for upcoming projects. During these meetings, the manager invites expressions of interest from staff to project manage key accounts. This small act offers employees diversity and choices in the work that interests them.

A Focus on Relationships

For many employees, commitment is fostered through healthy working relationships with colleagues and management. Anecdotal evidence suggests that one of the main reasons people leave a company is not inadequate pay or benefits; it is more often a difficult day-to-day working relationship with their immediate supervisor. The popular saying: "People don't leave organizations, they leave managers" is true a lot of times. Managers should acknowledge that a positive working relationship with an employee is one of the cornerstones of gaining commitment. Also, fostering supportive relationships among employees in a team or unit can engender a feeling of obligation to colleagues. Apart from the relationship with management, peer relationships can, and often do, have a major bearing on commitment.

Matching Individual and Organizational Values

The reconciling of employee and organizational values is another way of building organizational commitment. A good example of linking staff and organizational values occurs at *Medtronic*, the world's largest medical device company, headquartered in Minneapolis. Among many value-based initiatives, Medtronic regularly broadcasts to its 45,000 plus employees worldwide. The company shares stories of patients who have benefited from their medical products. Medtronic CEO Omar Ishrak states:

> The culture is one of the main reasons I joined Medtronic. It's highly customer-focused and highly mission-centric. Here is a company with a mission that hasn't changed in 50 years, and it's a great motivation for people to stay.[7]

Employees at Medtronic can "see" the end result of their work. Many of them are profoundly moved by patients' success stories. The matching of personal and organizational values builds and reinforces the desire to commit to the business's mission. Medtronic puts a human face on its mission, and has achieved employee-retention rates above the industry norm.

Of course, a company's mission is especially compelling when patients' lives are at stake. But companies in any industry can find creative ways to help employees understand and appreciate how their daily work has a personal impact on the lives of their customers. Employees in these circumstances commit to the organization because they *want to*. This strategy is very much in line with one of the dimensions of intrinsic motivation we discussed in the previous chapter: *purpose*. By according personal and organizational values, it engenders a sense of purpose and inspires intrinsic motivation.

Work–Life Balance

Another area impacting more and more on organizational commitment is the difficulties we all face trying to balance work and home responsibilities. Commitment can hinge, to a large extent, on putting in place flexible work practices to minimize conflict between work roles and home life. People are now defining their career success in terms of getting their work–home balance right—instead of climbing the corporate ladder. In an increasing number of people's eyes, hierarchical rank or status is less important than managing the duel responsibilities of work and home. Some companies are notable for their efforts in providing flexible scheduling, childcare facilities, and other support services, although most companies are still somewhat inflexible in work–life balance considerations.

Most companies these days have an overall policy for flexibly dealing with the complexities of their employees' time demands. But in practice, many managers are far less flexible in their interpretation of those policies than they ought to be. Future-oriented enterprises are more likely to develop comprehensive programs to assist employees in managing work–home conflicts, rather than cobbling together *ad hoc* experimental initiatives. After all, this shift is in keeping with the current realities of a market-driven workforce and the imperative to attract, keep, and produce committed employees.

> **Where the rubber meets the road ...**
>
> The following article was written by Nicola Middlemiss, a Canadian writer in *HC Online*:
>
> **Encouraging the elusive work-life balance—are we all talk?**
>
> Most employers encourage a healthy work-life balance but do we really mean what we say? One leading expert has suggested too many companies offer nothing more than lip-service.
>
> "I have a large amount of cynicism around the sincerity of many companies," admits management and strategy expert, Dr Linda Duxbery. "They talk balance but quite frankly they want people there and they want people working—it's shareholder value, its saving tax-payers' dollars."
>
> Duxbery is a noted pioneer in the field of organizational health and professor at the Sprott School of Business. She's earned a variety of awards that recognize her research, teaching and her contribution to public and private sector work places.
>
> According to Duxbery, "We've created a culture of the belief that the dedicated worker, the hard worker, the committed worker is the one who works the long hours and the people who push back are worried about getting ahead or even keeping their job in an environment like the one we have now."
>
> But Duxbery acknowledges that this is very likely going to change as millennials begin to make up the majority of the workforce.
>
> "They put a much higher priority on life," says Duxbery. "They've seen their parents on stress leave, they've seen their parents get divorced, they've seen their parents have drinking problems, on Prozac. They will not stay working for an organization that just gives lip service and doesn't provide balance."

> (continued)
>
> *Ahead of the trend*
> But not all companies can be branded with the same "lip-service only" label—HRM Online spoke to Julie Einarson, VP of culture and communications at *Benefits by Design*.
> BBD actively encourages all employees to pursue personal interests and offers two annual subsidies to every worker—one $200 grant to cover any costs related to health or fitness and a second to support non-sports related hobbies.
> According to Einarson, 93 percent of employees used the full subsidy on offer. "We're not just talking about these programs, we're actually making sure people use them," she insisted. "We have a commitment to promoting a healthy worklife balance," said Einarson. "Life shouldn't just be about work."
> BBD's work week is just 35 hours and every employee is given one paid day off a year to spend contributing to a charitable cause.
> Not only that, but the company encourages charity in-house too with back-to-school food bank drives and collecting shoes to ship to Haiti.
> "We give them ways to be involved," said Einarson. "It might not necessarily connect directly with the bottom line but we support them as individuals and help them make the world a better place."[8]

Given that business leaders are acutely aware of increasing worker mobility; it's difficult to gauge just how much effort and resources companies should put into encouraging organizational commitment. Notwithstanding this dilemma—and the fact that people are spending less and less time with the one employer—there are considerable performance benefits that come with building employee commitment. A committed workforce saves the firm money in the form of lower recruiting costs, fewer stranded clients, and less downtime. And knowledge sharing is diminished with higher than normal turnover of staff.

Business leaders should therefore be motivated to build employee commitment as a means to keeping some staffing stability, reducing costly turnover, and improving performance. Committed employees will also work harder and be more likely to "go the extra mile" in achieving business objectives. The self-motivated employee wants to exert their influence on business outcomes. The committed employee—one that doesn't necessarily want to hang around forever—wants to make a difference.

In a nutshell, increasing commitment—as distinct from promoting loyalty—is based on a number of factors, some of which we have already covered. These factors include, but are not limited to:

- sufficiency of pay, benefits, and rewards;
- family-oriented policies and actions;
- quality of the supervisory working relationship;
- relevance of learning and development opportunities;
- opportunities to be promoted;
- clearly stated and understood guidelines defining appropriate work behavior and job demands;
- participation in goal setting and strategic direction setting;
- receipt of regular, constructive performance feedback;
- supportive communications with immediate supervisors and upper management;
- procedural justice in promotional decisions; and
- evaluative and objective measures of performance.

Of course the reverse is true; commitment will surely erode if some or all of these factors are not addressed properly by business leaders.

Commitment is a two-way street between employee and employer. From the perspective of the employer, the key question is: *What can we as an enterprise do to help employees become more committed in assisting us to achieve our organizational goals?* And from a committed employee's perspective, the right response to this question is: *I'm willing to commit to these goals in return for the organization assisting me to achieve my personal objectives.* This transaction is part of a new psychological contract between the employees and the organization that we'll cover in more detail in Part III.

A committed employee is one who assists the enterprise in achieving its outcomes. The goal model of performance we covered in Chap. 1 is very appealing to the committed employee. This sense of commitment is realized when they either believe in the organizational mission; perceive a loss in leaving to work elsewhere; or feel a sense of obligation to the enterprise for helping them develop themselves and their career. Business leaders commit to assisting employees in achieving their personal objectives. This can be achieved by communicating the benefits of what the organization does for the community to create a better society, providing financial and social inducements to stay, and investing in resources to develop people. These individual and organization responsibilities are key to developing a culture of commitment over loyalty. Commitment is a significant driver of individual and organizational performance.

In Chap. 10, we examine the management myth that *a technically superior workforce is a pathway to a high-performing business*.

The Top 10 Key Points …

1. The loyal employee and the committed employee think differently. The loyal employee values the *status quo*; they like things the way they are; they don't like rocking the apple cart. The committed employee, to the contrary, welcomes change; they are more inclined to look for new ways of doing things, faster, better, and quicker; they will rock the apple cart, if they believe it'll improve things.
2. Human spirit describes the emotional connection to the work itself. Having a sense of commitment is tied to the employer; that's the fundamental difference between the values of human spirit and commitment.
3. It's in the best interests of the employee to seek commitment from their employer to support them in achieving their personal objectives.
4. One of the most notable models of commitment is John Meyer and Natalie Allen's; their model was developed to bring together the various definitions of commitment.
5. Meyer and Allen's model characterizes organizational commitment in three ways: a desire to stay, the cost of leaving, and a sense obligation to the employer.
6. An effective way of positively impacting more than one dimension of commitment is aligning career growth with company goals.
7. A job that offers variety and the freedom to make decisions and mistakes in a safe environment can engender commitment from the incumbent.
8. For many employees, commitment is fostered through healthy working relationships with colleagues and management.
9. The reconciling of employee and organizational values is another way of building organizational commitment.

10. Another area impacting more and more on organizational commitment is the challenge we all face in balancing work and home responsibilities.

Notes

1. Baker, T. (2014). *Attracting and retaining talent: Becoming an employer of choice*. London: Palgrave Macmillan.
2. Hamel, G. (2011). Three forces disrupting management. http://www.managementexchange.com/blog/three-forces-disrupting-management
3. The psychological contract is explained more fully in Chapter 12. In short, the psychological contract is the unwritten expectations employees and employers have of each other in the workplace.
4. Meyer, J., & Allen, N. (1991). A three-component conceptualization of organizational commitment. *Human Resource Management Review*, 1 (1), Spring, 61–89.
5. Meyer, J.P., & Herscovitch, L. (2001). Commitment in the workplace: Toward a general model. *Human Resource Management Review*, 11, 299–332.
6. Eisenberger, R., Fasolo, P., & Davis-La Mastro, V. (1990). Perceived organizational support and employee diligence, commitment, and innovation. *Journal of Applied Psychology*, 75, 51–59.
   Shore, L.M., & Wayne, S.J. (1993). Commitment and employee behaviour: Comparison of affective and continuance commitment with perceived organizational support. *Journal of Applied Psychology*, 78, 774–780.
   Wayne, S.J., Shore, L.M., & Liden, R.C. (1997). Perceived organizational support and leader-member exchange: A social exchange perspective. *Academy of Management Journal*, 40, 82–111.
7. Colvin, G. (2012). How to fix a great American business. http://fortune.com/2012/11/05/how-to-fix-a-great-american-business/
8. Middlemiss, N. (2015). Encouraging the elusive work-life balance—Are we all talk? http://www.hcamag.com/hr-news/encouraging-the-elusive-worklife-balance--are-we-all-talk-196257.aspx

10

Management Myth # 7—A Technically Superior Workforce is a Pathway to a High-Performing Business

Marcia faces a dilemma. One of her five production teams is performing well below her expectations. She ponders the array of options available to her to improve the team's performance. Is the poor performance due to a lack of technical know-how, she wonders. Could the problem be non-technical, such as a lack of team work? Could the substandard performance be about the team's inability to solve some of the challenging problems they face from the company's demanding customers? So many questions to consider.

Marcia considered that may be the lagging work performance could be resolved with personal rather than technical development. Or perhaps the solution is to learn some skills in dealing with out-of-the-ordinary problems the team is bombarded with from multiple stakeholders across and outside the company? In her mind, the first step is to investigate the matter further before considering her options.

After some careful thought and some further investigation, Marcia decides to apply three tactics to help the underperforming team improve its performance.

The myth that a technically superior workforce is a pathway to a high-performing business overrates job-centered training and underrates person-centered and problem-centered learning.

© The Author(s) 2017
T. Baker, *Performance Management for Agile Organizations*,
DOI 10.1007/978-3-319-40153-9_10

She plans to firstly do a skills audit on each member of the team. Once this training needs analysis is completed, Marcia will implement some technical training programs to boost the competency levels of individual team members, where needed. She hopes this approach will lift the performance in the team with the technical skill development of individual team members.

A second approach Marcia considers is to develop the non-technical capabilities of her team members. This approach is based on personal growth, rather than technical development. Using this strategy, she wants to use a team development workshop to build levels of trust and better communication between team members. No training in communication has previously been given to develop this team, Marcia acknowledges. This team was hastily put together, without any thought of how the individuals would work (or not work) together. Yet they relied upon each other to a great extent to exchange information and share resources. The team's interactions helped get the product out the door to the customer. This learning approach would focus on developing the members of the team personally, not technically.

Marcia's third tactic is to adopt a problem-solving approach to increase the team's decision-making capacity. A management strategy was proposed to review poor performance, including problem-solving and brainstorming meetings with—and between—members of the team. The complex nature of some of the problems meant the team sometimes took the wrong option under time pressure. This alternative adopts a "lateral thinking" approach to solve the myriad challenges confronting the team in their day-to-day dealings with other departments within the company and with stakeholders outside the business.

Each of the three approaches attacks the problem of poor performance from a different angle. One of these approaches—or a combination—is bound to work, Marcia thinks. She feels a renewed sense of confidence that the lagging performance issue can be fixed. By tackling the problem from several perspectives, it offers her a wider range of possible solutions to solving the learning and development issues within this poor-performing team. Using a multi-dimensional approach, Marcia comes to the conclusion that she has more chance of being successful in resolving a challenging performance management problem.[1]

The success of scientific management substantially relied upon teaching workers to comply with the one and only way of carrying out each job task. Learning was essentially based on technical training. In the early days of scientific management, non-technical development programs were non-existent and considered irrelevant. But today, learning and development programs that aren't job-specific are commonplace, although still overshadowed by technical training. The overriding type of workplace learning is still based on technical mastery of the job. This is the case, even though work performance extends past the boundaries of the job specification, as we discussed in Chap. 6. Technical job skills training therefore isn't the panacea for all performance issues. An overreliance on job-centered training can mean other viable non-technical learning and development options can be discounted.

The agile enterprise needs more than technical skill development to perform in our turbulent marketplace. Technical mastery, of course, is still important; it's closely aligned with the specialization and standardization of work. So it's understandable why technical training is the dominant mode of learning in workplaces. No one seriously disputes the value of technical proficiency in a high-performing workplace. But to survive and prosper, companies need non-technical proficiency too.

Across the spectrum of industries, employees are faced with a daily bombardment of problems, challenges, and dilemmas. Many of these predicaments can't be fixed with procedural knowledge and process skills learnt from technical training. As I've said a few times, thinking outside the box is the new norm. There's rarely a neat, prescriptive answer to resolving complex, left-field problems. The answers aren't always going to be found in the company procedure's manual.

More and more of these out-of-the-blue challenges facing people at work require thinking on one's feet. Technical training, as we discussed in Chap. 4, doesn't teach people to think laterally. Essentially, technical training does the opposite; it teaches trainees to follow procedures, processes, and systems. A key assumption supporting technical learning is that work situations are reasonably predictable and so can be resolved in a particular way, using a specific method. This idea is at the heart of scientific management and the stable and predictable marketplace it was borne out of.

With this explanation of technical training, I want to clarify the difference between training and learning and development. Training is a subset of learning and development; training is one of several approaches to learning and development. Furthermore, it's primarily concerned with enhancing the technical skill of the job-holder. Learning and development is a broader concept that takes into consideration both technical and non-technical dimensions of learning. Learning and development, being more comprehensive, covers many people development practices essential for building and sustaining organizational agility.

Consider the situation Marcia was put in at the beginning of this chapter. She wisely considered adopting a multi-dimensional people development perspective in overhauling one of her poor-performing teams. Marcia's plan included both technical and non-technical dimensions of learning. It makes sense to invest in a range of learning options to improve performance. Through combinations of technical and non-technical learning options, organizational leaders have greater scope for promoting agile performance. Putting it another way: The leader has "more strings to their bow" by applying a multi-dimensional learning and development approach to a performance situation. This multi-dimensional strategy shifts the emphasis from training to learning and development.

So in summary, the concept of learning and development is multifaceted. Training is one dimensional and one of several components of learning and development; its focus is substantially on technical skill development. Personal development and problem-based learning are the two additional dimensions that make up learning and development. Most workplace learning options can be classified as job-related, person-related, or problem-related. These make up the three dimensions of learning and development.

Of these three dimensions, the job-related component has been the more popular dimension since the beginning of scientific management. Work has transformed and so has the marketplace. We need to fundamentally rethink how we approach learning and development in light of this transformation.

As we know, performance at work is more than job mastery. As an illustration, being adaptable and enterprising are core contemporary competencies of high performers. These personal attributes are non-technical. A technical training program can't effectively teach people to be adaptable and enterprising. The agile enterprise needs a comprehensive interpretation of learning and development; one that's broader than the narrow, but nevertheless important, limits of technical training. Thorough technical training isn't effective for all performance matters in the workplace.

Apart from the indoctrination of Taylorism, the perspective a company takes in developing its employees says a lot about its collective attitude toward people. If people are viewed as a commodity, for instance, hired to help the company achieve its ends and nothing else, the development focus will surely be exclusively on technical training. At the other extreme, an employer who views employees as equal partners will be very receptive to a more eclectic approach to learning and development. This would include personal and career development opportunities. It's this collaborative thinking and the application of a balanced learning and development program that stimulates a culture of agility, enterprise, and adaptability. I have more to say about this is Part III.

So the three dimensions of learning and development can be expressed as:

- job-centered,
- person-centered, and
- problem-centered.

Each dimension has an apparent focus in its application. They separately emphasize a philosophical belief about development and have strengths and weaknesses. Briefly, the job-centered dimension focuses on technical training. The person- and problem-centered dimensions are non-technical in their orientation. Together, the three dimensions make up the multi-dimensional approach needed for agile performance.

Let's take a closer look at each dimension.

Job-centered

The most popular and conventional method overwhelmingly adopted by most organizations is *job-centered*. I'd guess 80 per cent or more of learning activities carried out in most organizations could be classified as job-centered.

This dimension emphasizes superior technical performance and skill mastery. The justification for expending money on building technical capacity is the tangible link between job skills training and job performance. So the primary motive is to develop the employees' job skills to directly improve performance on-the-job. Of the three dimensions, the job-centered approach is the one most directly related to the specifics of one's job performance.

Training programs, for example, that improve an employee capacity to operate a piece of machinery, to master some form of technology or a work-related system or process, are job-centered. These activities specifically relate to a job task an employee does. These training programs promise to be job-centered in their orientation. Successfully learning anything straight from a job-holder's job specification promises to have a direct pay-off in their increased job performance. Quality learning programs that are job-specific increase the employee's efficiency and effectiveness in their job role. The ultimate triumph of job-centered training is a more technically proficient employee. So it's pretty obvious why most enterprises invest heavily in job-centered training programs.

The employee benefits too, of course. Being technically proficient makes the job easier and reduces stress levels. Put simply, technical training assists an employee in performing their job with greater confidence and increased competence. Improved job performance often leads to promotion and more pay; it can, in other words, be beneficial career-wise. Job-centered training—attractive to both employer and employee—has many advocates who argue passionately for its virtues and application in the workplace, above the other two dimensions.[2]

Despite its popularity, a weakness of the job-centered approach is it primarily favors the interests of the organization over the interests of the employee. A predominantly job-centered training approach is based on Taylorism thinking that the employee is a small cog in the large-scale wheel of production. The employee is viewed as an abstract and anonymous job-holder or performer. The overriding expectation is that the employee passively reacts to stimuli in the organizational environment; there's little room for original thought or autonomy. Of course, it's true—as I pointed out—that the employee gains new skills that benefit them and their career. But job-centered training is based first and foremost on the needs and priorities of the business. The person doing the training is a secondary consideration.

Person-centered

The *person-centered* approach emphasizes self-development; it involves the employer investing in the personal growth of its employees, as people. While the job-centered approach is directly linked to job performance, the person-centered approach has a less direct link between the learning experience and job performance.

The motive for an enterprise sponsoring person-centered development is basically the same as the job-centered approach, but has a different impact. With the person-centered method, it's expected that the learning experience develops certain personal qualities in the employee's repertoire that ultimately improve their work performance. Unlike the job-centered approach, however, person-centered learning can indirectly—rather than directly—influence job performance. The person-centered approach is based on the idea that a more accomplished person can be a more accomplished employee.

Training programs that improve an employee's mastery of themselves—rather than mastery of a job skill—such as goal setting, personal motivation, time management, and emotional intelligence, potentially increase work performance in the right circumstances.

The incentive for an enterprise to sponsor personal development learning opportunities is to grow and nurture abler employees. Further, it is based on the belief that by developing the organization's more precious resource—its people—employees can be more efficient and effective in their work role. Over the past quarter of a century, the proliferation of personal development experiences, courses, and activities suggest this premise is well-founded.

> **Where the rubber meets the road ...**
>
> **Personal development learning in action**
> *Hillary Outdoors* (formerly *The Sir Edmund Hillary Outdoor Pursuits Centre of New Zealand*) was founded in 1972. The late Sir Edmund Hillary was involved as patron of the center. The vision of the center is to provide education by offering outdoor experiences to participants. People who engage in such adrenalin-producing activities tend to experience intrinsic changes. Positive gains are made in self-esteem, skills are developed, and social interactions are enhanced. Competition is subdued while cooperation is encouraged. A number of successful corporations have put staff and managers through outdoor programs such as those offered by the center. Through these experiences, participants explore values and recognize weaknesses and have the potential to create positive changes in themselves and their organizations.[3]
>
> There are many of these organizations around the world, based on personal development.

Aside from the organization, the people undertaking these programs potentially benefit the most. The opportunity to develop and improve and enrich their life and career prospects is appealing to most people. Personal development broadens the range of skills past technical capabilities. Of the two dimensions I've covered so far, the person-centered method—despite its growing popularity—is still a less appealing investment for organizational leaders. This is mainly due to the weaker connection between the learning experience and job performance.

But there's a subtle similarity between the job-centered and person-centered approaches. This connection is relevant when the organization is the sponsor. A person-centered learning experience is pursued—like the job-centered approach—in the interests of the paying organization first and foremost. The employee's needs—although not necessarily obvious on the surface—are a secondary consideration, in most cases. It's common practice for an employee, attending a personal development training program, to follow unquestioningly the direction of a trainer and the prescribed program. The course content is usually "cast in stone" and the trainer follows a predetermined pathway, regardless of the specific needs of the attendees.

It's typically the case that the trainee is given little option but to simply follow what the trainer says. Despite the rhetoric of "self-discovery," there is generally no real opportunity for the *participant* to engage in any real independent thinking in personal development programs. The trainee merely reacts to the direction set by the trainer and faithfully follows the sequence of activities in the training manual. Many personal development courses—like technical training programs—are "how to" or procedurally-driven learning experiences.

Take for example, the "Five Steps to Better Listening" communication program. The trainer typically leads the workshop participant methodically through these five steps—as entertaining and informative as it may be—throughout the duration of the program. I've no doubt this approach has merit; procedural knowledge gained this way is valuable and necessary for some life skills. However, too much attention on procedural training, in my opinion, undercuts the capacity for real personal development of a person. So, in more circumstances than may first appear obvious, the person-centered approach undermines the individual's fundamental and inherent self-determination.

Notwithstanding the organization-centric nature of job-centered and person-centered programs, they are valuable and certainly have an ongoing role in the performance-oriented enterprise. But these two dimensions and their programs reinforce the idea that the employer's needs take precedence over the needs of the employee.

Problem-centered

The *problem-centered* approach, the third learning and development dimension, is based on problem-solving; that is, being more effective at solving work-related problems. The focus of this approach is developing the employee's ability to analyze and resolve problems at work. With more capable problem-solving skills, people can make better decisions on-the-job. The argument for using this learning method is the direct and indirect connection between problem-solving capacity and performance. The primary motive for investing in problem-centered learning is to improve the employee's decision-making aptitude to cope with the escalating and unpredictable challenges they face in their work.

People are able to make better decisions in their day-to-day work if they have the necessary knowledge, skills, and attitude to deal with random problems, challenges, and dilemmas. Besides, with greater problem-solving capabilities, employees inevitably exercise greater autonomy in dealing with ambiguous issues affecting their work. This increased independence reduces the employee's dependency on their supervisor.

Topics such as creative problem-solving techniques, research skills, or analysis of real world case studies are examples of problem-centered learning.

It remains a mystery to me why this approach isn't more rampant in workplaces. When you consider the obvious relevance of problem-solving today, why isn't there more of this type of learning? When it's applied, this dimension of learning is based on the belief that by developing people's problem-solving capacity, it stimulates faster and better decisions.

What's more, you no doubt recognize *problem-solving* as one of the seven dimensions of organizational agility, which I covered in Chap. 3. And inevitably, quicker performance and better problem-solving will progress *customer responsiveness*; another core dimension of the Organizational Agility model. Apart from these obvious benefits, the more confident and self-sufficient someone is, the less the strain on their leader.

Like the other two dimensions of learning, the employee benefits from learning to problem-solve. Specifically, the incentive to learn better problem-solving skills is largely to be more autonomous. The employee is less reliant on their boss to make decisions affecting their work. You'll recall that *autonomy* is one of three intrinsic motivational forces we discussed in Chap. 8. The capable employee—one who can solve a wider array of work problems—has more freedom and greater assurance to make decisions and choices. Learning to problem-solve also enhances a person's employability prospects. Although slow to take hold—even with its obvious benefits—problem-centered learning experiences are gradually gaining prominence. The complex and less predictable working environment we face guarantee its ascendancy.

> **Where the rubber meets the road ...**
>
> **Problem-centered learning in the bank**
>
> Julie—executive manager of learning and development for a large, well-known bank—was charged with the responsibility of revamping the bank's approach to inducting customer service representatives (CSRs) in retail banking services. After looking at the turnover rates and gathering information from a series of conversations she had with CSRs and their managers, she decided it was time to act.
>
> From what she'd heard in these conversations, the bank had a challenge to reduce the high rates of turnover in CSRs in the first 12 weeks of their employment with the bank. Employees had told Julie in their conversations that they lacked confidence in their skills and product knowledge. Changing the learning approach in the induction program was the place to start, she concluded. Most of this training had in the past been too prescriptive and procedural and hadn't taken into account the ambiguous circumstances CSRs were often put in on the job.
>
> From a learning perspective, the new approach enabled participants to better analyze situations and source information more effectively. This policy, supported by a continuous coaching component, involved a partnership between the participant, their branch manager, and a "buddy" who was an experienced CSR. With this support, participants were required to take ownership of their learning and complete a series of tasks. In addition, they worked with their branch manager to identify strengths and areas of improvement through daily check-ins, debriefs, and feedback sessions.
>
> Collaborative learning occurs through the use of problem-based learning, simulations, and research. During the off-the-job learning periods, participants work in learning sets or groups and explore customer situations that they'd encounter in real life. They were encouraged to analyze the situation, explore how they would respond, and complete any customer transactions using simulations.
>
> To date, the CSR induction program has been able to deliver an 8 per cent reduction in voluntary turnover in the first six months of its inception.[4]

The problem-centered approach should be jointly considered and applied with the person- and job-centered perspectives. In the working environment we participate in, the ability to think laterally, creatively, and flexibly is paramount. Intense global competition puts pressure on treating every customer's request as exclusively as possible. This entails abandoning stock standard problem-solving approaches that frustrate the fickle customer. Being able to take an extraordinary situation and deal with it proficiently is a skills-set that benefits everyone: the customer, employee, and company.

The myth that a technically superior workforce is a pathway to a high-performing business overrates job-centered training and underrates person-centered and problem-centered learning. While personal development and problem-solving are well establish dimensions of learning, I think—as I alluded to earlier—they account for less than 20 per cent of learning and development expenditure. Which means, of course, that 80 per cent of many enterprise budgets are devoted to job-centered learning. Yet being agile depends, to a large extent, on non-job role performance (Chap. 6). It also relies upon the ability to solve problems quickly and successfully for the customer (Chap. 5). So my recommendation is to shift from a narrow job-centered focus to a multi-dimensional learning approach. Doing so, utilizes the strengths of all three dimensions of development.

A Multi-Dimensional Approach

There are strong advocates with compelling arguments for each of the three learning and development philosophies. And that's fine; they all have their place in organizational and individual learning. But each school of thought has its limitations too. So it stands to reason that the best learning and development strategy is multi-dimensional. An eclectic strategy is comprehensive and brings to light the value of each perspective. It's not really important which philosophical approach is the *best*; rather, a more constructive question for leaders to consider is: *What does each approach have to offer in improving performance?* Understanding and appreciating each dimension helps the leader to be more informed about their learning and development choices.

Take, for example, Murray, a team leader who's faced with the challenge of overturning lagging work performance in the team he leads. Murray can deal with this substandard performance in one of three ways, or apply a multi-dimensional approach. The performance issue could be tackled from a personal efficiency perspective. Using the person-centered approach, the key might be to improve the way Murray's team manages its workload. More specifically, the solution could be to train team members on how to manage themselves and their priorities more adeptly. By contemplating a time management program, Murray would tackle the performance issue from a personal development perspective.

Looking at the problem from another angle, Murray considers that poor technical competence is possibly the main reason for substandard performance. So a job-centered approach might be the best way forward to remedy any technical deficiencies within the team. Murray may decide that his team should undertake a competency-based training program, such as a course in administrative and clerical skill development. Raising the skill level of the team may lift performance.

Yet a third option open to Murray is to use a problem-centered approach. Consistent with this perspective, Murray considers facilitating a workshop on the problem of poor communication his team has with other teams within the company, and the further problems that causes. The purpose of the workshop would be to stimulate discussion on some of the key factors affecting the team's performance and particularly, how communication can be improved with other teams. Attacking poor performance from a problem-centered angle in this case means Murray wants to remove any internal communication barriers affecting team performance.

Any one of these three approaches, or a combination, could provide Murray with the answer to his poor performance dilemma.

A leader choosing from a range of different perspectives to solve performance issues has a broader set of options than simply defaulting to job-centered skills training. So a leader boosts their odds of resolving performance problems by adopting a multi-dimensional approach to learning and development.

To get the most out of learning and development to encourage agile behavior, I'd suggest one third of the organization's learning and development budget be allocated to each of the three dimensions I've covered. In practice, this translates to a third of the budget committed to the self-development of employees (person-centered approach), a third for specific training to carry out job skills (job-centered approach), and a third devoted to developing problem-solving capacity (problem-centered approach). This eclectic mix reinforces the legitimacy of learning and development as an enabler of higher performance; it balances the needs of individual and organization; and offers leaders more options for increasing productivity.

In the final chapter of Part II, we look at the eighth management myth that *employees can't be trusted with sensitive information.*

The Top 10 Key Points ...

1. Taylorism didn't see the relevance and need for non-technical learning and development programs.
2. Training is one approach of learning and development; it's primarily concerned with the technical skill enhancement of the job-holder. Learning and development is a broader concept, that takes into consideration both technical and non-technical dimensions of learning.
3. Most learning activities can be classified as job-related, person-related, or problem-related; the three dimensions of learning and development.
4. The job-centered approach is the one most directly related to the specifics of one's job performance.
5. Training programs that improve an employee's capacity to operate a piece of machinery, master some form of technology or a work-related system or process, are job-centered.
6. The person-centered approach is based on the idea that a more accomplished person can be a more accomplished employee.
7. Training programs that improve an employee's mastery of themselves—rather than mastery of a job skill—such as goal setting, personal motivation, time management, and emotional intelligence potentially increase work performance in the right circumstances.
8. A third learning and development dimension is problem-centered; that is, being more effective at solving work-related problems.
9. Topics such as creative problem-solving techniques, research skills, or analysis of real world case studies are examples of problem-centered learning.
10. The author recommends shifting from a mostly narrow job-centered learning focus to a multi-dimensional approach; this utilizes the strengths of all three dimensions of learning and development.

Notes

1. Baker, T. (2014). *Attracting and retaining talent: Becoming an employer of choice*. London: Palgrave Macmillan.
2. Kuchinke, K.P. (1999). Adult education towards what end? A philosophical analysis of the concept as reflected in the research theory, and practice of human resource development. *Adult Education Quarterly*, 49 (4), 148–160. Maitland, I. (1994). The morality of the corporation. *Business Ethics Quarterly*, 4, 445–458.
3. http://www.hillaryoutdoors.co.nz/about/
4. Baker, T. (2013). *The end of the performance review: A new approach to appraising employee performance*. London: Palgrave Macmillan.

11

Management Myth # 8—Employees Can't Be Trusted with Sensitive Information

Rachel received a phone call from an irate customer. *"Your last invoice overcharged me on my telephone account by $149.90. I'm not happy about it and want it fixed straight away!"* demanded Charlie Robertson, the fuming customer.

"Okay Mr Robertson, let me bring up your account details on my screen; I won't be a moment," replied an anxious Rachel.

"Yes, there appears to be a mistake Mr Robertson, according to our records. I'll need to talk to my manager about this and get back to you," Rachel responded, with a touch more confidence.

"Why do you need to talk to your boss if it's obvious that you have made a mistake in your billing?" demanded Charlie, in an intimidating tone.

"That's company policy, Mr Robertson," came the meek response.

Once off the phone, Rachel immediately went to speak with Margaret, her manager, about Mr Robertson's situation. Margaret looked at Rachel and

---

Although today's knowledge worker is exposed to more information—and has a greater expectation to be kept informed—there's still a lingering attitude that divulging too much information to employees is counterproductive.

said, after momentarily studying the information on the screen of her computer, "Obviously there is an error. Call Mr Robertson back immediately and let him know that we'll credit him this amount in our next invoice."

Just as Rachel was about to leave her manager's office, Margaret said, "Okay, let's set a rule here, Rachel. From now on, if a customer calls and complains, and it's obvious that we have made an error and it involves a sum of $200 or less, then I want you to fix it straightaway without consulting me. That way, we're unlikely to antagonize the customer any more than necessary. I want you to show initiative in future under these circumstances. Okay?"

Rachel called the customer back to reassure him. Charlie Robertson responded with, "Thank you, but I don't understand why you needed to talk to your manager if the situation was obviously a mistake."

Rachel felt a little more empowered now, knowing that her boss wanted her to show initiative if a billing error in future was less than $200. Although feeling more confident, Rachel hoped that this kind of error wouldn't occur again.

When it comes to sharing information, many managers operate on two false assumptions. They assume that employees can't be trusted with sensitive information. These traditional managers believe that there is a high risk that employees will pass confidential information on to an inappropriate source outside the organization, such as a union. The belief is that managers are more trustworthy than employees with confidential company information. Management can, in other words, be trusted not to misuse information, but employees can't. In reality, managers are no less or more trustworthy than employees.

There are, of course, many more employees than managers and perhaps with larger numbers, the potential for the abuse of this information is greater. But the idea that employees are less trustworthy is obviously complete nonsense. Harboring this false belief is not lost on employees; they know that withholding information from them is symptomatic of a lack of faith and trust. This assumption erodes trust levels even further and has a negative effect on the collaborative working relationship fundamental for cultivating agile behavior.

The second incorrect assumption is that information can be controlled by withholding it. This belief is flawed for two reasons. First, information vacuums are quickly filled with some sort of information—whether accurate or not—which can be more damaging than sharing the correct information in the first place. And second, social media puts paid to the idea that you can completely control the flow of information. People "talk" via social media. So instead of trying to contain information, managers should do the opposite; that is, increase the flow of information throughout the enterprise.

The only information a worker was exposed to on the Ford Motor Company assembly line—or any other company in the early part of twentieth century—apart from gossip, was work instructions. Specifically, this information entailed what was expected of the worker in performing their job. The boss didn't want to confuse workers with anything that wasn't directly related to their work. The familiar adage: "you'll get told on a need to know basis" probably originated in this era.

Although today's knowledge worker is exposed to more information—and has a greater expectation to be kept informed—there's still a lingering attitude that divulging too much information to employees is counterproductive. It's too risky; employees can't be trusted with information that's not job-related, is still a predominant belief. It's certainly no coincidence that one of the biggest gripes employees have about management across nearly every industry is that they are frequently "kept in the dark"; they aren't told what they ought to be told.

Restricted communication channels have a negative effect on the business's capacity to be agile. Employees need exposure to more and varying types of information to know with confidence *when*, *how*, and *why* they need to be adaptive, flexible, and customer-focused. Even though knowledge workers have access to more information than employees 100 years ago, it's still usually not enough to perform with optimum agility.

Taking stock for a moment; so far in Part II, I've suggested that employers need employees who:

- are willing to flexibly deploy their skills-set;
- are customer- and performance-focused;
- are keen to work in project-based teams when needed; and
- feel engaged, committed, and open to growing and developing.

But many of the antiquated performance management practices enduring from scientific management foster the opposite characteristics. Specifically, the principles of scientific management encourage employees to:

- specialize rather than deploy their skills-set;
- have an internal- and job-focus rather than a customer- and performance-focus;
- be more functionally-based than project-based;
- be merely satisfied rather than engaged with their job;
- display loyalty but not necessarily commitment; and
- be technically-trained and ignore their non-technical development.

And as we cover in this final chapter of Part II, scientific management encourages closed rather than open channels of communication; yet another impediment to agility.

When it comes to information, the productive knowledge worker wants and needs:

- the opportunity to work in a variety of work-settings;
- to be equipped with the necessary information, skills, and incentives to focus on the customer;
- to be recognized for good performance;
- to contribute constructively to cross-functional projects;
- to undertake meaningful work;
- to exchange their labour and expertise for personal and professional opportunities to grow and develop; and
- to have access to a wide range of helpful information in order to act with initiative and autonomy.

I cover the requirement to act with initiative and autonomy in this chapter.

All of these factors are reliant on the communication of information. Employees need access to a wide array of information channels to accomplish the agility requirements I've covered in Part II.

For starters, the agile enterprise supports their workforce with a constant flow of information about organizational direction, market requirements, product and service updates, and new systems and processes. The spread of information enables the employee to be adaptable and enterprising at the right time, in the right way, and in the right place. Effective communication, in all its forms, "takes two to tango." In response to helpful information, the employee is expected to show initiative; in other words—to be fully involved in the processes of decision-making in the business.

While the value of this exchange is well understood, adopting the practices to enable two-way communication entails a massive shift in thinking and behavior for many enterprises. The orthodox practice is to be selective about the type and detail of information shared with the workforce. *You'll be told on a need to know basis*—is still pretty much the norm. In response to these carefully managed information channels, the average employee is understandably reactive and compliant. They do what they're told.

Controlled information flow makes displaying initiative too risky. In a communication void, the employee is reticent to be enterprising. At the other end of the spectrum, having access to plentiful, accurate, timely, and useful information stimulates enterprising action.

I'd like to explore this link between information and agility further. There's a commercial advantage in having open channels of communication. More decisions can be decentralized with a plentiful supply of information, particularly at lower levels of the organization (Chap. 2). Enabling more employees to make more decisions in more places in the business, eases management pressure; leaders can attend to strategic matters. There are employee advantages too; knowledge workers want and need autonomy in carrying out their work, as we covered in Chap. 8.

As I've said quite a few times in *Performance Management for Agile Organizations*, businesses profit from flexible, adaptable, and responsive organizational structures. These attributes are the product of a culture of shared ideas and information. It's the opening—not restricting—of information networks that enables greater involvement from more people in all functions of the business. The agile enterprise is a dynamic organism, growing, flexing, and changing in response to the demands of its surrounding environment. This is in direct contrast to the staid, dull, corroded, and inflexible bureaucracy harboring restricted informational channels.

Pick up any book or article on change management and it'll stress the relevance of information within and beyond the business. Authors like me love to write about the necessity of clear, frequent, and honest communication between employer and employee. This is because open information is a vital and widely discussed ingredient of a vibrant, healthy organization.

What's more, there's a renewed interest in participative values and practices. As business tries to come to terms with the hyper-competitive, "twenty-four seven," VUCA market, it's looking to involve everyone in solution-finding. But a more collaborative approach to decision-making only works with open dialogue between employer and employee.

Open communication has important consequences for attraction and retention, for instance. Top talent doesn't welcome being told what to do; they want freedom and autonomy; they want to be proactive and part of the decision-making process. Attracting the right people and retaining the ones already employed, depends, as much as anything else, on the health of the employment relationship. And the state of the employer/employee relationship is dependent on the quality of internal communication.

All these factors I've covered here, legitimize a policy of open communication to fuel agile performance.

> **Where the rubber meets the road ...**
>
> **Tapping into employee knowledge as the engine for growth**
> Manufacturing steel cans is a mature industry. *Brasilata*, the Brazilian company has figured out how to tap into employee knowledge and motivation to fuel its extraordinary productivity and innovation. It has won top industry and supplier awards almost every year, including the coveted Sherwin-Williams "Best Packaging Supplier" award. It has also been ranked among the 20 most innovative companies in Brazil, as well as one of the best places to work in that country.
> Innovation drives change at Brasilata. At the heart of the company's business model is the *Simplification Project* (Projeto Simplificação), which encourages all 900 employees across the company's four production facilities to think up as many suggestions as possible. "The Simplification Project

> (continued)
>
> is like panning for ideas (incremental innovations), thereby stimulating the internal innovative environment and entrepreneurial spirit," explains Brasilata's CEO, Antonio Carlos Álvares Teixeira.
>
> Ideas are so important that Brasilata employees are called "inventors," and everyone signs an "innovation contract" that reinforces their commitment to continuous improvement. After a slow start two decades ago (with only one idea per person each year), the company now receives more than 200,000 ideas each year—an average of more than 220 ideas per employee. Brasilata holds a party every six months, at which all employees celebrate teams and individuals with the best ideas. Employees are also rewarded with bonuses representing 15 per cent of net annual profits.
>
> Some employee suggestions have sown the seeds of innovative products, such as an award-winning paint can that can withstand heavy impact when dropped. Other ideas have dramatically improved productivity. Some changes have made jobs redundant, but employees aren't worried. Brasilata has been able to maintain a no-layoff policy even during the worst downturns.
>
> Brasilata's success is also built on teamwork. The company compares its workforce to a soccer team, in which winning goals depends on everyone. "Teamwork is one of the leading forces of the company," says the company's website. The company also emphasizes employee initiative and open communication. "In our opinion, innovative action is stimulated by a corporate environment where the communications channels are always open, new ideas are respected and errors tolerated."[1]

Initiative Paradox

A big trap that interferes with initiative is what researcher David Campbell refers to as the *Initiative Paradox*.[2] As a consultant, I get this question all the time: *How do we get our employees to show more (or any) initiative?* I think the frustration managers have is mostly to do with the way this initiative paradox works.

I have illustrated the paradox in Fig. 11.1.

Here is my explanation of the how the initiative paradox works. At the outset of a new organization, leaders and team members are "on the same page." The leader wants each team member to exercise appropriate initiative. And team members are willing to be proactive and enterprising in the right circumstances.

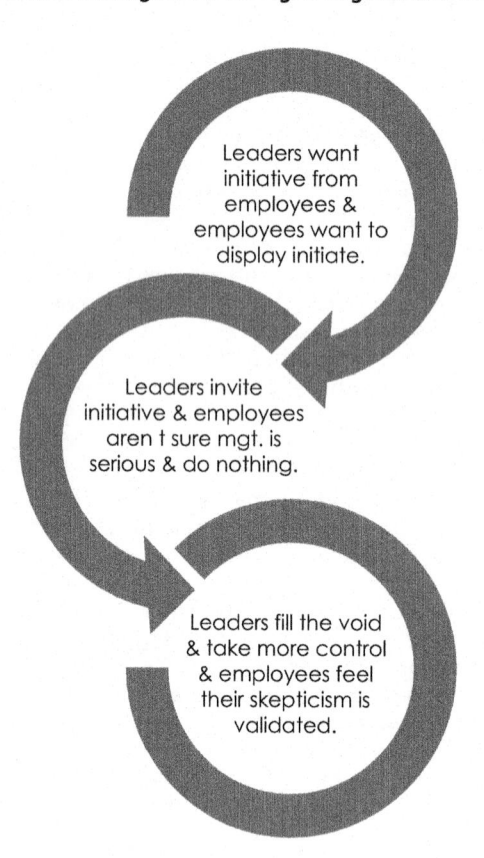

Fig. 11.1 Initiative paradox

Leaders consequently urge their team members to act with initiative. But team members are skeptical; they aren't too sure whether the leader genuinely wants them acting in enterprising ways. So team members play it safe and elect not to be proactive; they instead rely on their leader to give them direction.

The leader observes this reactive behavior and infers that team members don't really want to be proactive or show initiative. They become frustrated with this lack of enterprise. This reactive behavior results in the leader rushing in and being more directive and autocratic than they intended in the first place. Team members observe what they interpret as micro-managing from their leader. This directive leadership behavior validates the team member's initial skepticism. The team member assumes, in other words, they were right in their original judgment; that is, management wasn't really serious about them displaying initiative. And now, it's the employees' turn to feel frustrated. So the initiative paradox is based on misunderstandings—and the reinforcement of these misunderstandings—about the motives of the other party in the employment relationship.

Enabling employees to make enterprising decisions—as complex as it seems from the initiative paradox—is nevertheless the cornerstone of agile performance. The challenge of resolving this initiative paradox involves greater numbers of employees and their managers across more and more industry groups than it did in the twentieth century. The key to unlocking this paradox is communication; more specifically, removing communication barriers between leaders and team members.

Better communication means equipping employees to be more knowledgeable, self-sufficient, participative, adaptive, flexible, efficient, and responsive to their rapidly changing surroundings. As I reiterate, employee collaboration is well understood, if not well practiced. Facilitating employee initiative is a perennial challenge for organizational leaders across all industries.

The crux of the problem is this: *How does the leader encourage team members to express their initiative when it is required? And simultaneously, how does the leader ensure the same people follow company guidelines and processes when needed?* Managers have used many tactics to resolve the initiative paradox; company rules have been introduced, the workplace regulated, policies formulated, and guidelines offered. Some tools have worked, but most have failed.

I'm sure you can think of examples where you've observed too much initiative—or more likely—other occasions where not enough enterprise was shown. Getting the balance right is more difficult than it appears.

Let me illustrate the initiative paradox in a typical scenario.

Consider a retail franchise business. Employees will often talk about "ownership," when they refer to their involvement in a retail outlet. These shop bound employees are probably multi-skilled or flexibly deployed in all the tasks and activities involved in running the retail operation. These same employees typically question what they think is needless interference by head office in the running of *their* store. This "intrusion" may involve such things as policy making, customer interaction, purchasing, stock control, and implementing new systems and procedures. Head office's involvement, more often than not, causes tension in the retail outlets.

Based on head office input, employees in the stores assume that their initiative to make decisions is being sabotaged. And because employees think there's unnecessary interference in their day-to-day store operations, they are less inclined to be proactive. Management observes this lack of resourcefulness; they assume that employees in the stores can't, or won't, act with initiative when needed. Head office becomes irritated with frontline employees, whom they think are too reliant upon management to make simple operational decisions. So management reluctantly feels justified in making decisions in operational matters. This vicious cycle leads to negative feelings all round.

So how is the cycle broken?

According to David Campbell, there are four practical strategies that help to overcome the initiative paradox and open the lines of communication between employees and management. These are:

- goal alignment,
- boundary refinement,
- sharing information, and
- active accountability.[3]

Let's take a look at each of these strategies.

Goal Alignment

Goal alignment means bringing into line the perspectives of employees and management. Where there's agreement between the objectives of the two parties, it minimizes the possibility that employees won't be in conflict with their manager, when exercising their own judgment. Without goal alignment, employee initiative isn't always going to be welcomed by management. The assumption supporting goal alignment is that conflict isn't the result of the enterprising qualities of employees *per se*; rather, it is the outcome of a misalignment between organization and individual.

When misalignment occurs between a team member and their leader, it often causes confusion and conflict. Take, for instance, the case of a company that openly espouses *transparency* and *honesty* as important values to guide behavior. But the senior executive team of this company holds lots of secretive meetings behind closed doors. Information from these meetings is withheld from employees—no minutes are taken or disseminated. It's also observable that some of the relationships in this team are fractured and interactions are often characterized by mistrust. Under these circumstances, transparency and honesty are hardly likely to be practiced regularly by employees. It is quite possible that this example will foster the opposite values of secrecy and untruthfulness.

So one of the simplest—yet most neglected—ways of bring about goal alignment between management and employees is leaders "walking the talk." If members of the executive team consistently demonstrate transparency and honesty in their dealings with each other and the organization-at-large, the rest will most probably follow suit. The result: alignment between organization and individual.

Here is a subtler illustration of goal misalignment: Samantha sends a mixed signal during a casual discussion with Dominic, one of her team members. On the one hand, she insists that Dominic keeps her well informed about all his interactions with a difficult customer. On the other hand, Samantha reminds Dominic to use common sense and show initiative with this customer, when he needs to. When informed later about Dominic's proactive approach with this particular customer, Samantha chastises him for taking that action. This confuses Dominic. If Samantha criticizes his actions without first praising Dominic for taking some initiative, he justifiably interprets this as criticism for being proactive. The outcome is *goal misalignment*, the opposite of what Samantha wants.

Some practical measures leaders can take to align the goals of employees and employers are:

- Putting in place a clearly-defined performance bonus system to reward and encourage alignment.

- Managers setting an example or walking the talk.
- Consistent informal dialogue between managers and team members.
- Performance feedback conversations that focus on aligning individual and organization goals.

Boundary Refinement

Boundary refinement is a second way of overcoming the initiative paradox. This involves carefully communicating the kind of initiative the leader expects and doesn't expect. This means, in other words, communicating the extent and limits of an individual's authority to be enterprising. Explaining when and where enterprising behavior is welcome and unwelcome clarifies the boundaries of proactive behavior. On the contrary, if boundaries aren't communicated, employees are likely to be confused and hesitant about displaying initiative. The assumption underpinning this strategy is that in certain situations it is appropriate and expected that initiative be taken. But in other situations, it's inappropriate to show initiative.

Given the complexities of organizational life, boundary refinement is often easier to suggest than to accomplish. Nonetheless, when an employee is confused about when or where to show initiative, it's often because their leader has not clarified and communicated the boundaries. So in practice, boundary refinement is a never ending dialogue between leader and team member.

It's an ongoing conversation because these boundaries continually change; they change over time, sometimes rapidly without warning, and in different circumstances. A leader eager to empower team members, is aware of these changing conditions, and is hasty in communicating their renewed expectations, when they arise. Apart from regular dialogue, the effective leader uses a variety of tactics to communicate shifting boundaries. Team meetings and discussions, critical incidents and their lessons, coaching and clarification, and email and written instructions, are the main methods.

I'll illustrate two of these methods used in combination: the team meeting and critical incident. Consider a common dilemma facing an airline company: an incident where an airplane has been grounded with unforeseen mechanical difficulties. What are the roles and responsibilities of airline personnel when this scenario inevitably occurs? To clarify and communicate the appropriate boundaries in this predicament, a leader can organize a series of workshops to discuss a recent aircraft grounding incident. The workshops can comprise a cross-section of the company, including pilots, flight attendants, engineers, customer service representatives, salespeople, and operational crew. In discussing this scenario in the workshops, the focus should be on boundary refinement; that is, clarifying and understanding the roles and responsibilities of all employees. How does each functional area communicate and minimize the passenger inconvenience, while ensuring safety standards are upheld? The ultimate aim is getting the plane airborne as quickly as possible. In other words, recovery speed— one of the seven dimensions of agility—is the challenge in this case (Chap. 3). This problem-centered approach (Chap. 10) encourages the workshop participants to elucidate when and where they should perform to resolve this common, but unfortunate, scenario.

The boundary refinement strategy works by limiting employee initiative to very specific and clear instances. So it's particularly attractive to the leader who feels uncomfortable relying too heavily on people's independent judgment, though less appealing to a leader who wants employees to use their initiative expansively.

Some practical measures that can be taken to communicate boundaries for displaying proper initiatives include:

- Using critical business incidents to illustrate and clarify boundaries for proactive behavior.
- Coaching and mentoring employees in their work.
- Documenting acceptable and unacceptable forms of initiative.
- Rewarding and emphasizing appropriate initiative.

Sharing Information

Sharing Information builds trust. This strategy concentrates on minimizing unshared expectations between employer and employee. By providing everyone working in the enterprise with the same information, perspective, and frame-of-reference, expectations are consolidated. This basically means that management and employees are "on the same page." The underlying assumption is that by sharing the right information, trust builds and employees gain a similar outlook to management on a range of important business matters. This strategy welcomes enterprising behavior through a steady and proper flow of information from organizational leaders. Sharing information is particularly useful for strategic planning and business improvement.

To illustrate my point, Bob using the services of a professional and independent facilitator for his team's annual retreat. This meeting is an opportunity to exchange important information. The primary purpose of this retreat is to develop, evaluate, and modify the team's five-year plan, involving everyone. Bob begins the retreat by sharing his vision, mission, and values with the whole team, inviting them all to work collaboratively to develop a structured five-year plan. In other words, the facilitator works with the team to develop a series of goals that are in line with Bob's vision. Bob's team subsequently works with the facilitator to create a series of strategies, plans-of-action, accountabilities, and timelines to meet these goals. This cooperation encourages everyone in Bob's team to be involved in—and initiate—big picture planning.

Bob always gets great value from these retreats; the sharing of information exercise puts all team members on the same page. This common understanding instills confidence in Bob's team members to take the necessary initiative to achieve shared goals and milestones.

Another practical, simple, and effective information sharing exercise can be used to improve the business. Allison invites her team to explore ways and means of being more efficient and effective. She asks her team to identify one area that needs improving within the team's span-of-influence. It may involve doing things faster, easier, safer, with better quality, or improved communication. Several issues are put on the table for consideration. Allison then asks the team to vote on the issue they believe to be the most pressing or relevant for the team to resolve. Collaboratively, the team decides their number one improvement priority and then gets to work. A continuous improvement plan is then developed and documented. Again, by freely exchanging information, this continuous improvement plan aligns the perspectives of everyone in Allison's team.

In these two examples, Bob and Allison are essentially sharing their managerial role with all members of their team. Throughout the process, team members gain a better insight of their manager's thinking on important issues, procedures, and priorities. This alignment begins with the leader freely sharing work unit information and strategies with colleagues. Such openness exposes the leader somewhat; they become more reliant on their team members to get the work done. However, as I've indicated, the strategy elevates higher levels of trust between leader and team.

Some key steps you can take to share information include:

- Holding annual strategic planning days.
- Running continuous improvement workshops.
- Facilitating group problem-solving sessions.
- Running regular team discussions.

Active Accountability

Active accountability involves an understanding between the manager and employee that initiative and independent judgment can be exercised, but only at the risk to the employee. If the outcome of an employee's initiative, in other words, is unacceptable to management, it can be detrimental to the initiator. This strategy is characteristic of bureaucratic and authority-focused organizations, such as the military. Organizations of this ilk rely on a clearly-defined chain-of-command to make decisions. The underlying assumption here is that there is scope for displaying initiative; but the initiator is ultimately accountable for their own proactive actions.

Consider Marco; he's in-charge of purchasing stock in a large corporation with very stringent purchasing rules and regulations. One of the company's policies is to order in stock in the last week of the month. But Marco has advance notice that his company has won a large contract with a big customer. This customer requires immediate delivery of the product.

It's the beginning of the month. Marco decides to place the order early in the month in response to the immediate needs of the customer. This enterprising behavior violates a major company policy. But by taking this initiative, Marco delights the customer with quick responsiveness; and management don't feel the need to criticize Marco for this agile behavior.

Here is another example in a military environment.

Max—a squadron leader—refuses to comply with an illegal order from Joe, his direct superior. Specifically, Joe orders Max to cover up the details of a murder before the official investigation takes place. By not following orders, Max is violating a command from his superior officer, Joe. While the subordinate may suffer initially for insubordination from his commanding officer, Max doesn't undergo negative consequences outside the confines of the military unit. Officers beyond Joe's command are supportive of Max's stance on this matter. In these types of circumstances, the organization generally wants employees to use their independent judgment, but only on the basis that the organization treats an error of judgment harshly.

As you can probably appreciate, this strategy is the least effective of the four approaches for promoting employee initiative. It does, however, have its place. Active accountability is different from the other three strategies in that it doesn't specify the conditions when initiative should take place. Yet it's acknowledged that exceptional circumstances—such as the examples above—may call for initiative to be shown and the rules bent.

Uncertainty around whether to bend the rules or not means people will understandably hesitate before taking proactive action. And if their subsequent actions cause a problem, it's easier for the leader to blame the proactive person for not following rules and protocol. Under these conditions, the employee can't be certain the organization will back their judgment and actions.

Active accountability means decisions are evaluated dynamically. This assessment is done case-by-case, with the benefit of hindsight of the ultimate outcomes of the proactive behavior. The benefits are weighted heavily in favor of the organization; there are few benefits for the proactive employee, especially when poor judgment is exercised! Active accountability will, in most cases, discourage—not encourage—agile behavior, except in extraordinary circumstances.

Here are some circumstances where active accountability may be considered a useful communication strategy:

- Conducting workplace investigations.
- Showing initiative against unethical behavior.
- Reporting unlawful behavior.
- Crisis management.

By using these four communication strategies, the leader can overcome two significant roadblocks in conquering the initiative paradox. The first is enticing the employee to exercise autonomous decision-making that benefits the business. Understanding that varying circumstances require different forms of initiative (and compliance) is the second challenge. Each strategy tackles these circumstances in different ways, and together offer a useful framework for evaluating workplace situations that require enterprise.

Each strategy also attempts to curb unwanted initiative. Boundary refinement and active accountability do this by confining enterprising behavior to certain situations. Goal alignment and sharing information encourage suitable initiative by fostering a common perspective between the employee and their manager. So undesirable proactive behavior should be more apparent using these two strategies. In any case, leaders should think carefully about when and where they can use each of these communication strategies to overcome the initiative paradox.

In conclusion, these four strategies place limits on undesirable forms of initiative and at the same time encourage initiative in desirable or—at least—tolerable ways. The common thread in these four strategies is open communication. To encourage and support proactive, agile workplace behavior, leaders need an open and continuous dialogue with their team members. This communication framework endeavors to improve and refine the flow of information. It's not just the business that benefits from open communication. Employees benefit also by knowing where and when to be involved in exercising suitable agile behavior.

This completes Part II of *Performance Management for Agile Organizations*. We've covering the eight management myths originating from scientific management that hold businesses back from being agile and nimble in the marketplace. Each of these myths supports performance management practices that are polar opposite to the practices needed for stimulating workplace agility. Apart from attempting to debunk these eight myths, I've offered practical alternatives—based on a different set of beliefs—that promise to facilitate the dimensions of agility we covered in Part I.

In Part III, I want to bring the threads together into a coherent framework to strategically manage the cultural transformation from scientific management to agile performance.

The 10 Key Points …

1. There is a prevailing myth that employees can't be trusted with sensitive information; the risk is they may pass this information on to inappropriate sources.
2. The initiative paradox is a misunderstanding, due to a lack of communication between management and employees, that results in limiting enterprising behavior from employees.
3. The first of four ways of resolving the initiative paradox is goal alignment, which brings into line the perspectives of employees and management.
4. Some practical measures leaders can take to align the goals of employees and employers are: putting in place a clearly-defined performance bonus system to reward and encourage alignment; managers setting an example or walking the talk; consistent informal dialogue between managers and team members; and performance feedback conversations that focus on aligning individual and organization goals.
5. Boundary refinement is a second way of overcoming the initiative paradox. This involves carefully communicating the kind of initiative the leader expects and doesn't expect.
6. Some practical measures that can be taken to communicate boundaries for displaying proper initiatives are: using critical incidents in the business to illustrate and clarify boundaries for proactive behavior; coaching and mentoring employees in their work; documenting

acceptable and unacceptable forms of initiative; and rewarding and reinforcing appropriate initiative.
7. Sharing information is the third strategy in overcoming the initiative paradox. This strategy concentrates on minimizing unshared expectations between employer and employee.
8. Some key steps you can take to share information include: holding annual strategic planning days; staging continuous improvement workshops; facilitating group problem-solving sessions; and running regular team discussion meetings.
9. Active accountability is the fourth and final way to deal with the initiative paradox; it involves an understanding between the manager and employee that initiative and judgment can be exercised, but only at the risk to the employee.
10. Some circumstances where active accountability may be considered an appropriate communication strategy are: conducting workplace investigations; showing initiative against unethical behavior; reporting unlawful behavior; and crisis management.

Notes

1. Kristy. (2015). Case study: Tapping into employee knowledge as the engine for growth. https://www.thinkbusinessservices.com.au/case-study-tapping-into-employee-knowledge-as-the-engine-for-growth/
2. Campbell, D.J. (2000). The proactive employee: Managing workplace initiative. *Academy of Management Executive*, 14 (3), 52–66.
3. Ibid.

Part III

The Right Culture for Agile Performance

12

A New Psychological Contract for Managing Agile Performance

Maryanne, a new employee, was being inducted into the company and trained by Marco, a long-time member of a customer service team. As the new member of the team, Maryanne appreciated Marco's experience and knowledge. She quickly gained a reasonable level of confidence in her new role. One thing she also rapidly learned was that a key performance measure was how quickly visitors were processed, not how well their inquiries were handled.

"It feels like churn and burn," Maryanne told Marco. "Lots of these people are coming back again and again with the same issue and they're upset at us for not giving them the right information. It seems like we should be spending more time finding out what the real issue is when they first come in." "Not our problem," fired back Marco. "That's the manager's problem. They just don't want to see lines of people."

Although Maryanne wasn't content with this response, she persevered with things until she took complete ownership of the role and then started engaging with customers to try to prevent repeated visits and provide better service.

The most profound influence on culture and its traits, is the relationship between the owners of the business and their agents—management—and employees of the business.

"You're taking too long with the customers," Maryanne was told by Tom, her manager. Explaining her rationale and commitment to deliver better service was to no avail. *"That's not your concern,"* Maryanne was told.

Where do I begin? might be a question you're asking yourself at this stage. *What's my first step in managing the performance of the agile enterprise?* Good question. I've thrown a lot at you in *Performance Management for Agile Organizations*.

We've traversed the evolving methods of the way performance in organizations has been evaluated for the past 100 years. The only method of evaluating performance pre-1950s was via profit margins. Enterprise agility is now the key indicator of performance. We then covered the common characteristics of an agile organization. From here, we explored the dimensions of agility. Although I define seven distinct dimensions, each dimension is interconnected to other dimensions in the model, to some degree. With a comprehensive understanding of agile performance, we then explored the main barriers to agility in Part II. These obstacles are eight management myths about performance. I offer some practical solutions to overcome these roadblocks. These management myths were fortified by the scientific management movement, beginning in the early part of the last century. A serious rethink of performance management is in order after 100 years of indoctrination.

Part III contains one chapter—this one. Its intention is to tie the many threads together into a coherent framework. Furthermore, the framework serves to pinpoint the necessary changes required to remove these antiquated management ideas about performance. The framework illustrates the kind of workplace culture conducive for agility to flourish. The pivotal feature of this culture is a new psychological contract between employer and employee.

A culture of agility—based on eight shared values between employer and employee—is diametrically opposite to the traditional psychological contract, based on the principles of scientific management. The culture suited to scientific management is one that safeguards the consistency and efficiency of production lines. But the management beliefs and their supporting practices impede the creativity and flexibility necessary to survive and thrive in the changing world of work.

These scientific management principles and practices—once the solution for high performance—are deeply entrenched in our thinking. Today, we still operate on these beliefs, even though our understanding of performance is drastically different. Instead of helping, these practices are now thwarting performance, principally agile performance. The eight management myths we covered in Part II, instinctively embedded in the psyche of management and employees, go unchallenged for the most part. Scientific management principles are still unquestioningly practiced, even though knowledge work needs to be managed entirely differently. The framework in Part III juxtaposes the old and new cultures and their performance management practices.

Let me be clear about this: This shift from the old to the new isn't merely about implementing a few new performance management tools. The new tools I covered in Part II aren't sustainable—unless the workplace culture changes to accommodate them.

When I refer to *culture*, what do I mean? Workplace culture in my opinion hinges on the prevailing generic psychological contract between employer and employee. Without changing the contract, behaviors and practices will, before too long, revert to the old ways. People's actions ultimately will be consistent with the working relationship underpinned by the traditional contract. This longstanding psychological contract is the foundation for a simple, clear, and stable working environment. In this contract, the demarcation of managerial and worker responsibilities is apparent. But we need a culture that's befitting a complex, ambiguous, and ever-changing working environment. This calls for a fundamentally different kind of working relationship between manager and employee.

So the missing piece of the cake—and it is a large slice—is a new model of the manager/employee working relationship; the cornerstone of an agile workplace culture. The alternative performance management tools we've discussed, need to be introduced in a culture receptive of agility and its dimensions. This new ethos must be initiated by management. But its success very much depends on a cooperative partnership between employer and employee.

There are myriad definitions of workplace culture. Perhaps the most down-to-earth way to describe workplace culture is the *way things are done in a workplace*. The way things are done covers everything from the uniform people wear to subtler cues, such as the way people contribute (or don't) in meetings. People are immersed in the culture. It usually takes an "outsider"—someone who isn't part of the culture, or a new employee—to pick up the understated cultural cues.

So where does culture come from? I think it comes from many inputs, both within and without the organization. But I think the most profound influence on culture and its traits, is the relationship between the owners of the business and their agents—management—and employees of the business. It's the interaction patterns between organizational leaders and organizational members that shape the way things are done more than anything else.

For example, if there's a fairly distant and formal working relationship—based on hierarchy—between management and workforce, then this permeates the artefacts, beliefs, and practices of the culture. Uniforms will visibly reflect rank. Managers will be addressed formally and distinctively. And meetings are probably characterized as reporting mechanisms, devoid of collaborative dialogue, stringently adhering to a rigid written agenda.

At the other end of the spectrum, an organization without a high power differential will function completely differently. In this *laissez faire* environment, it's going to be more difficult to distinguish leaders from team members. The leaders, for instance, may not have offices. Everyone is probably on first name basis, including the CEO; sometimes people's nicknames are used. The meetings are more casual and decisions arrived at more collaboratively.

So workplace culture is very much a by-product of the employment relationship. And this employment relationship is shaped by a dominant psychological contract. What's a psychological contract? *Psychological* means that it is in the mind rather than written down. *Contract* means it's an agreement between two or more entities, in this case two. Put simply, a psychological contract is the unwritten expectation both entities have of each other in the employment relationship.

Figure 12.1 is a simple illustration of the psychological contract.

Even though they're not documented, the two sets of expectations (employee and management) shown in Fig. 12.1, are just as compelling—if not more so—as any written document. For instance, at its most basic level, managers expect employees to turn up to work punctually and do a solid day's work. And for this, employees expect that they'll be treated fairly and paid on time for the work they do. There are many collective expectations such as this that make up a psychological contract.

A psychological contract—like all contracts—can be broken. If an employee habitually turns up late to work, for instance, this behavior violates a management expectation. Or if an employee is underpaid, paid late, or not paid at all, this will undermine an employee expectation of the employer's obligation. Once the contract is broken, it negatively impacts the working relationship. Trust is eroded.

These psychological contracts can be strengthened too. When employees are meeting basic management expectations by consistently turning up to work on time and putting in a decent effort, their behavior reinforces in the minds of managers that employees are fulfilling their obligations. This builds trust; matching expectations buttress the contract; in this case, in the manager's mind. When expectations are met, or not met, in the minds of both parties, it strengthens or weakens the main psychological contract.

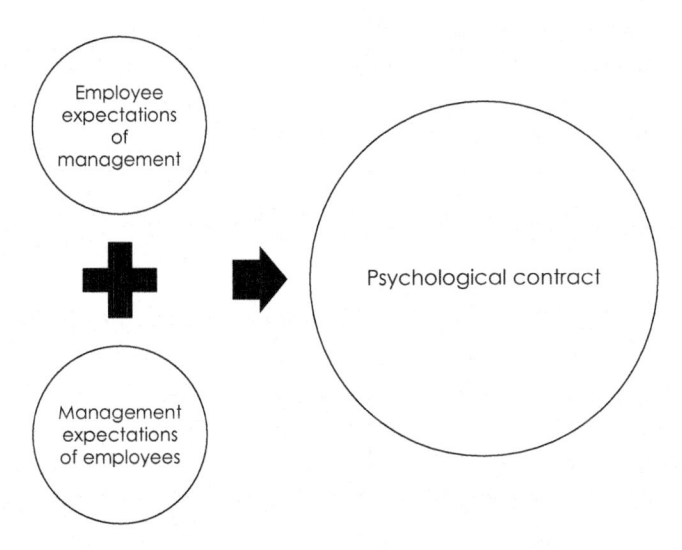

Fig. 12.1 Psychological contract

The Traditional Psychological Contract

With more than 200 years of conditioning—and principally with the influence of scientific management—a common psychological contract has developed and fortified. Two centuries of industry and the philosophy supporting scientific management have given durability and oxygen respectively to the management myths we've covered in Part II.

Scientific management and the traditional psychological contract have a symbiotic bond. On the one hand, scientific management strengthened and entrenched the existing psychological contract. The expectations and pivotal values of the conventional employment relationship was a product of the Industrial Revolution. Scientific management is a natural extension of the conventional employment relationship; its values and principles are compatible. So it's comprehensible that scientific management grew and took hold in industry. On the other hand, when scientific management became mainstream, it reinforced the traditional expectations of employer and employee.

Before defining this traditional psychological contract, I'd like to point out that these frameworks I'm about to share with you are an extension of my previous work on the psychological contract. The research started with my doctoral study and was further developed in my first book: *The 8 Values of Highly Productive Companies*.[1] The employee and employer expectations and the shared values are the same as my original model. But I've subsequently included the matching management myth in Table 12.1 and the new management belief in Table 12.2.

Table 12.1 shows the amended traditional psychological contract framework.

Referring to Table 12.1, the first column, labeled *Management myth*, covers the false beliefs we discussed in Part II. The second column is the value management and employee share, based upon the corresponding myth. These shared values are pivotal to the generic psychological contract. In the final two columns, I summarize the expectations management and employees have of each other, relating to the shared value.

Specifically, the third column summarizes the manager's expectation of an employee. And the last column is the employee's expectation of management. These expectations are nurtured by the myths arising from the principles of scientific management.

This framework summarizes the management and workforce expectations of the eight myths blocking agile performance in Part II. In other words, management myths are put into the context of the traditional psychological contract. Transforming organizational culture to enable the seven dimensions of agile performance I outlined in Chap. 3, starts with an evaluation of the psychological contract. The employment relationship is the backbone of organizational culture.

To change the culture, we need to understand what the ideal culture ought to look like. Table 12.2 is an illustration of a new psychological contract suited to agile performance.

You'll note that the column headings are the same as those in Table 12.1, except for the first column. There are eight corresponding rows juxtaposed against the beliefs and values of the traditional psychological contract framework in Table 12.1.

I want to devote the rest of the book to describing these *management beliefs* and how they are polar opposite to those eight management myths underpinning the traditional psychological contract. Further, I'll consider the matching shared values and expectations in how they benefit the dimensions of agility. Table 12.2 is an exemplar of the psychological contract necessary for agile performance. It represents an ethos where management and workforce work together in the opposite way to the old generic psychological contract. To attain these markers in the new framework, a completely different belief system to the one that supports the eight management myths is required.

Meeting the descriptors in the new psychological contract framework involves a dramatic change of thinking about the working relationship from both entities. One party may change, but if the other party's mindset won't—or can't—change, the culture won't budge. One partner changing their outlook without the other will produce conflict, confusion, and misunderstanding. And if the culture doesn't shift to reflect the

Table 12.1 Traditional psychological contract framework

Management myth	Shared value	Management expectation of employees	Employee expectation of management
Job specification improves performance	Specialized employment	• *Work* in a clearly defined & specialized employment area	• *Offer* clearly defined & specialized employment opportunities
Quality systems & processes guarantee good outcomes	Internal-focus	• *Follow* organizational policies & practices	• *Support* employees to follow organizational policies & practices
The job description helps the employee understand their organizational role	Job-focus	• *Fulfill* job requirements	• *Link* rewards & benefits to fulfilling job requirements
A business is best organized around functions	Function-based work	• *Focus* on job functions	• *Structure* work around functions
A satisfied employee is a productive employee	Human dispirit & work	• *Value* a stable & secure job	• *Offer* stable & secure jobs
A loyal employee is an asset to the business	Loyalty	• *Display* loyalty to employer	• *Reward* employees for displaying loyalty to the organization
A technically superior workforce is a pathway to a high-performing business	Training	• *Commit* to gain technical qualifications	• *Provide* opportunities to develop technical skills
Employees can't be trusted with sensitive information	Closed information	• *Comply* with managerial instructions	• *Provide* sufficient information for employees to do their job

Table 12.2 New psychological contract framework

Management belief	Shared value	Management expectation of employees	Employee expectation of management
Flexible deployment improves agile performance	Flexible deployment	• *Willingness* to work in a variety of roles & settings	• *Offer opportunities to* work in a variety of role & settings
An external focus produces good outcomes	Customer-focus	• *Serve* the customer before your manager	• *Provide* support & incentives to focus externally
The role description helps the employee understand their organizational role	Performance-focus	• *Perform* job & non-job roles	• *Provide* support to focus on performing job & non-job roles
A business is best organized around functions & projects	Project-based work	• *Willingness* to contribute cross-functionally as well as functionally	• *Provide* opportunity to use skills & gain experience working in project teams
An engaged employee is a productive employee	Human spirit and work	• *Valuing* work that is meaningful	• *Provide* work (wherever possible) that is meaningful
A committed employee is an asset to the business	Commitment	• *Commit* to achieving the business goals	• *Commit* to assisting employees to achieve their personal & career objectives
A multi-dimensional approach to learning & development is a pathway to higher performance	Learning & development	• *Commit* to lifelong learning & development	• *Support* for technical and non-technical growth & development
Enterprising behavior comes from open channels of communication	Open information	• *Willingness* to show enterprise & initiative in the right circumstances	• *Providing* access to a wide range of information

> **Where the rubber meets the road …**
>
> **Misalignment of expectations**
>
> Indira is an employee with an expectation that as part of a team she will be consulted and involved in decision-making from time-to-time on work-related issues. Further, Indira believes that Roslyn, her manager, ought to share the responsibilities for decision-making with her team. But in this case, Roslyn has a different understanding of the psychological contract. Roslyn thinks that the lines of responsibility between herself and her team are very clear. In Roslyn's mind, her managerial role is broadly to make decisions and the team member's job is to follow her instructions and carry out the work.
>
> Indira finds it exasperating that Roslyn in unwilling to engage the team in discussions. She's keen to discuss her ideas with Roslyn. But Roslyn is not at all receptive to any of her ideas or suggestions. Roslyn doesn't believe in collaborative leadership. She views her role, and the role of all management, differently. Roslyn thinks her role is to be decisive and to communicate those decisions clearly to employees. Roslyn thinks of this as being accountable and professional. Indira labels this mindset as "command and control."
>
> These conflicting unwritten expectations result is some real frustration between Roslyn and Indira, despite the fact that both are, in their own ways, trying to fulfill what they understand to be their responsibilities.

framework, the practices we covered in Part II may work initially, but over an extended period of time, they won't be viable.

I now want to consider each value in the new psychological contract framework. I'll refer to each value and how it promotes agility with reference to the seven dimensions of agility. All eight of these shared values in Tables 12.1 and 12.2 have either a direct or indirect, negative or positive impact respectively on the Organizational Agility model in Fig. 3.1 (Chap. 3).

Flexible Deployment

Flexible deployment (Chap. 4) is the capacity to apply a specific set of skills in a variety of ways. This value is the basis for several performance management strategies. Approaches such as job rotation, job enlargement, job enrichment, and multi-skilling are flexible work practices. It can also mean physically moving from one location to another, such as a transfer or secondment. The performance management tool I suggest to strengthen flexible deployment capability is based on multi-skilling, using a skills matrix.

Having an internally mobile workforce is essential for organizational maneuverability. Being able to deploy a set of skills in an assortment of ways boosts the employee and enterprise's capacity to adapt. Further, the deployment of people's skills in a variety of contexts makes a business less vulnerable to sudden fluctuations in the economy. Having the ability to use their skills in a range of ways, benefits the employee by maintaining their currency and employability. So this flexible work practice benefits both employer and employee.

What's more, flexible deployment has a positive effect on all seven dimensions of agility. But of them all, flexible deployment is crucial for a business's maneuverability and adaptability—the ability to *change direction*. Having the capacity to move employees around the business easily and from one set of tasks to another with minimum disruption, is an adaptive advantage. *Specialized employment*—the opposite value—makes changing direction a very difficult feat.

Another bonus of role rotation is that the rotated employee views their new tasks through a fresh set of eyes. Without fixed ideas that accompany the customary working arrangements of specialization, a flexibly deployed employee has a fresher perspective; they're more prone to query and critique existing practices. Specialization, and the narrow focus it engenders, inculcates a rigid set of beliefs about how things can and should be done. Specialists, through habit and familiarity, naturally uphold and defend established processes and procedures.

Conversely, a flexibly deployed employee is inclined to ask questions such as: *Why do we do things in this way?* So dimensions of agility such as *innovation, processing,* and *recovery speed* can benefit from a new and constructively critical perspective. The dimensions of *problem-solving* and *continuous improvement* also profit from a fresh outlook and new ideas.

Customer-Focus

The underlying thinking of *customer-focus* is that everything thought about, said, and done in the business, should have the customer in mind. In practice, it means that all decisions, business activities, and processes that take place throughout the business are planned, executed, and evaluated in the context of the customer and their needs. Customer-focus supports people development practices such as clarifying roles, providing incentives for focus on the customer, administering good support systems, and more (Chap. 5). Although a seemingly simple idea, customer-focus is an elusive value; but one that's essential in the hyper-competitive global marketplace we live and work in.

As I've said several times, the twenty-first-century customer is fickle, demanding, and has an abundance of options available to choose from. It's impossible for any enterprise to perform without at least sufficiently satisfying the customer. Being able to dealing effectively and responsively with customers are skills and outlook that are in great demand across all industries. So it's in the career-conscious employee's interests to be customer-focused.

Being customer-focused relates to all seven dimensions of agility. But the obvious dimension it applies to is *customer responsiveness*. To be truly responsive, the employee's attention has to be external, the opposite of the corresponding value of *internal-focus*. To be outwardly focused, a company needs a quality customer relationship management (CRM) system in place. The CRM system captures what the customer is thinking and what they are doing with the products and services they purchase. Being customer responsive means using a combination of human and technical assets.

A focus on the customer can accelerate the speed of *innovation, processing*, and *recovery speed*. A customer-focused manager or team member will actively consider new and improved goods and services, and how best to make them accessible to the customer before their competitors. Having an internal-focus, with its concentration on business processes, may devalue or miss opportunities to develop better products and services.

Being customer-focused puts a different slant on processing speed too. Internal-focus considers a process in terms of how it benefits the business. Whereas, having a customer-focus means considering a process in terms of how it best supports the customer.

Finally, the speed of recovery is likely to be faster with a focus on the customer. An internal orientation in comparison, encourages an attitude of apportioning blame and searching for fault in systems and processes. This is usually done before responding to the disadvantaged customer. An internal-focus slows, not increases, the speed of recovery from a mistake.

Performance-Focus

Performance-focus—as distinct from a *job-focus*—espouses a holistic perspective on performance. It takes into account job and non-job dimensions of performance. The job description by its definition covers the job role only. As I indicated in Chap. 6, significant non-job roles, such as positive mental attitude and enthusiasm, aren't usually spelt-out in a job description. But non-job roles are of paramount significance to agile performance.

An agile enterprise is going to be fueled by positive energy; it's is doubtlessly team oriented; it's likely to stress employee development; and it's continuously improving. These attributes are additional to the technical requirements of job tasks. An employee dedicated to performing these non-job roles is an asset to any business. Just as the customer-focused employee is in greater demand, so too, the employee prepared to perform these non-job roles.

Of the seven dimensions of agility, the two most apparent beneficiaries of a performance-focus are *innovation* and *continuous improvement*. Two of the four non-job roles directly relate to personal and organizational development—the career and innovation and continuous improvement roles. While the career role stresses personal improvement, the innovation and continuous improvement role underscores workplace improvements.

Within the new psychological contract framework, managers expect employees to contribute to workplace improvement. *Job-focus* as a value, on the other hand, de-emphasizes organizational improvement and development. The employee's main responsibility is limited to carrying out their job specification to the best of their ability. Under the old contract, workplace improvement is considered the responsibility of management. And without involving all members of the organization, the speed of organizational development can be slower and less effective.

A job-focus can mute the speed of processing too. Concentrating wholly on their job, the employee is blasé about opportunities to speed up work processes outside the realm of their work description. But in a culture that values total performance, the employee is more attuned to systemic issues beyond the scope of their job, such as improving the speed of processing.

Project-Based Work

Project-based work is completely different from *function-based work*. Work structured around disciplines is function-based and work structured around projects is cross-functional (Chap. 7). Cross-functional work draws on expertise from several disciplines within the business. I've suggested that balancing functional and cross-functional work structures enables organizational agility. If managed skilfully, drawing together diverse views, perspectives and expertise can challenge conventional thinking and lead to new ideas and better business outcomes.

What's more, agile performance is derived from improving the quality and quantity of cross-functional communication. The free exchange of information across functional boundaries provides a channel for swapping ideas and sharing perspectives. Fresh thinking and disparate views drive adaptive behavior and agile performance. Employees benefit too. When exposed to greater variety—working alongside colleagues harboring different thought processes—employees grow and develop.

Project-based work structures facilitate rapid direction changes. Function-based work structures—in comparison—are notoriously sluggish and indifferent in times of change. Changing direction is substantially more awkward with rigid, top-down hierarchical organizing structures. These obsolete organizing structures grew out of specialization.

Apart from nimble maneuvering, cross-functional project-based work inspires creative thinking. The cross-pollination of ideas and viewpoints is the lifeblood of improvement. Diversity in a team, particularly a cross-functional project team, challenges entrenched and fixed positions and fosters new lines of enquiry. This powers new products and services and encourages constructive critique. Function-based work, instead, breeds uniformity; everyone belonging to the same department tends to accede to established conventions and beliefs. This sameness suffocates creative thinking.

Human Spirit and Work

Human spirit and work is concerned with tapping into the employee's intrinsic motivation. The knowledge worker, as I pointed out in Chap. 8, responds best to three dimensions of motivation: having some autonomy to make their own decisions; understanding the bigger purpose of what they do; and being given an opportunity to develop their skills-set. Reward and punishment; that is, extrinsic motivational tactics still have their place—particularly when it comes to unskilled and semi-skilled workers. But for the skilled worker, extrinsic rewards, such as adequate pay and conditions, won't engage human spirit with work. An agile workplace is likely to be characterized by a core of intrinsically motivated individuals.

Furthermore, a highly motivated workforce is resilient, adaptive, and flexible in the face of a hyper-competitive and tumultuous marketplace. Companies are screaming out for employees who are enterprising, able to think for themselves, understand the bigger picture, and want to master their craft. Using a competitive salary and good working conditions to generate excitement and enthusiasm never was—and never will be—the ultimate motivational force.

Innovation and *processing speed, continuous improvement,* and *problem-solving* are dimensions of agility that directly profit from engaged employees. An intrinsically motivated employee will, for instance, question the relevance of work practices used. If necessary, the engaged employee then will search for new and better ways to get the job done. *Why are we doing it this way? Is there a better way?* are the questions they think about. Instead, a satisfied employee isn't as enthusiastic to take ownership of improving workplace methods.

Mastery—one of the three dimensions of intrinsic motivation Dan Pink speaks about in his book, *Drive*—is also a type of improvement. The quest for mastery involves continuously improving oneself; in a word, self-improvement. Self-mastery and refining the business environment is characteristic of a high-performing business. It gives the enterprise an *edge*. To have this competitive edge, a company needs a critical mass of employees with their human spirit invested in their work. A dispirited employee, or even one that's reasonably satisfied, won't have the same intrinsic drive for self-mastery.

People with their human spirit nourished by the work they do is an obviously benefit. They enjoy coming to work, being productive, and having resilience—all attributes that most of us seek in ourselves and others.

Commitment

In Chap. 9, I conceptualized *commitment* as a pragmatic exchange between employee and employer. More specifically, the employee commits to assisting the business achieve its objectives. And in return for this, the organization commits to assisting the employee to further their personal and career aspirations. This is different from *loyalty*. Loyalty is more idealistic; it is based on the notion that the employee is beholden to their employer all their career—or at least for a sizable chunk of it. In return for this display of loyalty, the employer looks after that employee with preferential treatment over the less loyal employee. Loyalty is not necessarily useful—and can even be counterproductive—when it comes to agile performance.

The committed employee—the one who doesn't expect, nor wants to stay employed in the one company for a long time—is doubtlessly more receptive and open to change. If change helps the business attain its goals, the committed, rather than the loyal employee will probably be more enthusiastic about it. A loyal employee is liable to defend present practices; their loyalty is probably to the practices of the company over business outcomes. A committed employee is a natural fit for an agile enterprise.

Rapid change is challenging for the loyal employee. The employee, loyal to their employer, is naturally protective of their familiar surroundings; they want things to remain as they are; they are resistant to sudden and large-scale change. A committed employee, with no such sense of loyalty, is more amenable to changing direction and letting go of past practices and rituals that are roadblocks to progress.

Ironically, a loyal employee may not be as responsive to customers as they ought to be. The loyal employee with their extended employment with the company, probably has reasonably good working relationships with several of the company's loyal customers. But in the event of a dispute between the customer and organization, the loyal employee will instinctively side with the business. Their company loyalty may blindside them from considering how they can still be responsive to the needs of the customer without any negative consequences to their employer. A committed employee has a better attitude in responding to a customer need, whether that need is in conflict with the business's policies, or not. Being committed to the goals of the organization, this employee will probably consider all options to satisfy the customer without sabotaging the company.

With career and development opportunities offered by their employer, the committed employee can advance their career, either with their current employer, or a subsequent employer. Contrariwise, a loyal employee's career can be stunted with a longstanding employer. They may not get the growth and development needed to advance their employment prospects elsewhere, or even internally.

Learning and Development

Learning and development, as I defined it in Chap. 10, is multi-dimensional; it's more than *training*. The value of learning and development covers technical-, person-, and problem-centered dimensions. Training, on the other hand, is exclusively focused on the technical-centered approach. Whereas learning and development is all-encompassing.

Organizational development and multi-dimensional learning go hand-in-hand. By concentrating entirely on the technical dimension, all the work-related predicaments people face won't be addressed by training. The comprehensive value of learning and development supports both the individual and organization to meet the countless challenges they face in a dynamic environment.

For example, innovative thinking is encouraged with an emphasis on person- and problem-centered learning. These kinds of learning supplement technical-centered training, which primarily teaches people to comprehend and follow formulaic processes and procedures. Of course, this type of learning has its place. The prescriptive approach, however, doesn't teach in-depth divergent thinking and creativity. With exposure to the other two dimensions of learning, the employee can learn to solve problems and develop personally. This multi-dimensional learning experience helps to stimulate the outside-the-box thinking that's indispensable for agile performance.

Because technical training teaches the trainee to follow proven processes and procedures, they don't learn to fully scrutinize these practices. Exploring ways to speed up, eliminate, or change established systems isn't usually part of the training curriculum. So person- and problem-centered approaches counterbalance technical training.

Technical-centered training does help to resolve conventional problems quickly. But technical training may be useless in recovering from out-of-the-ordinary mistakes. A speedy recovery, for instance, often needs some creative thought; the sort of thinking taught in problem-centered learning. So technical training is not a panacea for all technical dilemmas.

Besides the business, the employee benefits from a multi-dimensional approach to growth and development. They improve their employability and it opens up opportunities to capitalize on their strengths and innate talents outside the scope of the job specification.

Open Information

Open information, as we discussed in the last chapter of Part II, is concerned with initiating an information channel that encourages and equips employees to perform in proactive ways. There are four strategies to overcome what's referred to as the initiative paradox. These strategies are goal alignment, boundary refinement, sharing information, and active accountability.

At the other end of the communication spectrum, *closed information* is based on the misguided belief that employees can't be trusted with sensitive information. Conservative and risk-adverse managers favor restricted information channels when communicating to employees. This information vacuum, however, is a substantial liability in promoting enterprising behavior.

Agile performance is ignited by timely, relevant, regular, and shared information between managers and employees. This exchange of information is ultimately about ensuring that the employee and their boss have a similar outlook on the direction the enterprise is heading. Clarity of purpose means the employee feels comfortable exercising their initiative; they have a better understanding when and how this can be achieved. Acting in a non-prescriptive and proactive way is a fundamental attribute of agility.

All seven dimensions of agility are enriched when suitable initiative is exercised. The employee who is encouraged and prepared to be enterprising is receptive to new ideas. They're more open to look for ways of improving systems and processes, solve problems with a degree of creativity, and genuinely respond quickly to the needs of the customer. With communication barriers, the employee understandably sticks to the "official" process or protocol; in short, they play it safe. This compliant employee can then defend their actions and point to "doing things by the book."

We've all been on the receiving end of someone saying in their defense, "I'm simply following the rules and regulations," when a situation calls for using initiative, much to our frustration. Compliance—rather than creativity—is the safer route, at least in the mind of the employee in these risky situations. This means that when there is uncertainty about displaying initiative, the methods and procedures the business uses takes precedence over achieving business outcomes. Open dialogue and a free exchange of information between the manager and employee can break this dependency on safety and compliance.

Apart from the company, employees benefit too. They're more engaged, feel confident to be proactive, and are more accountable for their own behavior. These benefits unquestionably increase their intrinsic motivation and enjoyment of their work, and eventually this should benefit their career.

In summary, as I said at the outset of this chapter, cultivating a culture that dramatically reworks the dominant psychological contract is the key to managing ongoing agile performance. I've provided you with a framework based on eight shared values of the culture conducive to stimulating agile performance. So the obvious question now is: *Where do I start?*

The starting point is to evaluate the current organizational culture, using the frameworks in this chapter. Once the culture has been benchmarked, you can then implement some of the strategies I have shared with you in Part II. What you implement first will depend largely on the results of your evaluation and the priorities of the business. Start with one value.

By successfully changing one of the eight values, you'll simultaneously shift other values. These eight values are integrated. For instance, by flexibly deploying the skills of a workforce (flexible deployment), new skills are required (learning and development). Or, by shifting from a function-based to cross-functional organizing structure (project-based work), this affects non-job roles such as the team role (performance-focus). If you'd like more information on the tool I've designed to benchmark organization culture, take a look at one of my previous books—*Attracting and Retaining Talent: Becoming an Employer of Choice*,[2] or contact me directly.[3]

At any rate, I wish you well on your journey to managing agile performance.

The Top 10 Key Points …

1. The most profound influence on organizational culture and its traits is the relationship between the owners of the business and their agents, management, and the employees of the business. It is the interaction patterns between organizational leaders and organizational members that shape the culture more than anything else.
2. The new psychological contract framework consisting of eight values is juxtaposed against the traditional psychological contract framework to provide the necessary indicators for culture transformation.
3. Flexible deployment is the capacity to apply a specific set of skills in a variety of ways.
4. The underlying thinking of customer-focus is that everything thought about, said, and done in the business should have the customer in mind.
5. Performance-focus—distinct from a job-focus—espouses a holistic perspective on employee performance.
6. Balancing functional and cross-functional work structures enables organizational agility.
7. Human spirit and work is concerned with tapping into the employee's intrinsic motivation.
8. Commitment is a pragmatic exchange between employee and employer; the employee commits to assisting the business achieve its objectives and the organization commits to assisting the employee to further their personal and career aspirations.
9. The value of learning and development covers technical-, person-, and problem-centered dimensions.
10. Open information, as we discussed in the last chapter of Part II, is concerned with opening an information channel that encourages and equips employees to perform in proactive ways.

Notes

1. Baker, T. (2009). *The 8 values of highly productive companies: Creating wealth from a new employment relationship*. Brisbane: Australian Academic Press.
2. Baker, T. (2014). *Attracting and retaining talent: Becoming an employer of choice*. London: Palgrave Macmillan or go to http://winnersatwork.com.au/organisation/ at the Corporate Culture Change Cycle.
3. I can be contacted at tim@winnersatwork.com.au

Index[1]

A

absenteeism, 63, 149
accountability, 61, 102, 108, 114, 122, 123, 184, 189–93, 215
adaptive advantage, vii, xi, 5, 46, 71, 99, 123, 132, 207
adaptive behavior, 63, 78, 210
adaptive leadership, 53, 55n8
advisors, 14
agents, 14, 82, 85, 200, 217n1
Allen, Natalie, 147, 157
alliances, 23
Amazon, 23
ambidextrous, 81, 86
ambiguity, 28, 34, 94
apple, 21, 35n1, 40, 41, 122, 157n1
assembly line, viii, 61–3, 90, 128, 130, 177
assessment tools, 150, 151
attraction, x, 180
Australasian Legal Practice Management Association, 37
autonomy, 27, 77, 116, 128, 130, 134–6, 138, 139, 151–2, 165, 168, 178–80, 211

B

baby boomer, 59, 132
balanced score card, 13
Barnes, Andrew, 37, 38
Barnes & Noble, 23, 24
belief system, 131, 203
better decisions, 167, 168
blueprint, 91
bonus pay, 133, 136

---

[1] Note: Page numbers followed by "n" denote notes

Borders, 23, 24, 35n2, 37
boundary-spanning role, 82
Buddhism, 132

C
Campbell, David, 181, 184
career, 31, 50, 59, 85, 101, 103, 104, 106n9, 140n3, 142, 144, 145, 150–1, 153, 156, 157n6, 163–6, 205, 208, 209, 212, 213, 216, 217n8
career benefits, 145
career coaching, 151
career development, 101, 103, 104, 106n9, 144, 150, 163
career development opportunity, 103
career prospects, 50, 166
centralized power, 28
chain-of-command, 25, 109, 110, 118, 189
change direction, 24, 51, 52, 64, 80, 207
change management, 30, 31, 180
Chartered Institute of Personnel and Development (CIPD), xi, 66, 72n4
closed system, 6
coaching, 65, 68, 69, 82, 151, 169, 186, 187, 192
commercial advantage, 179
commitment profile, 149
committed employee, 143, 155, 156, 157n1, 205, 212, 213
communication barriers, 172, 183, 215
communication channels, 33, 44, 48, 111, 115, 177
communication skills, 70, 109
company goals, 150–1, 157n6

company performance, vii
company restructures, 41
competency, 69, 70, 93, 97, 106n1, 160, 171
competing values model, 16, 18, 19n9, 19n10, 38, 81
competitive advantage, 61
complex adaptive system, 6, 12
complexity theory, 18
compliance, 16, 40, 83, 86, 87n9, 136, 191, 216
Confucianism, 132
consultants, 7, 14, 38
Contingency planning, 53
conversations, 7, 59, 60, 169, 186, 192
creative thinking, 94, 211
crisis management, 191, 193n10
critical incidents, 186, 192
cross-functional communication, 44, 108, 110, 111, 115, 210
cross-functional projects, 31, 32, 35n7, 83, 103, 108, 109, 119, 121, 135, 178, 211
cultural transformation, 192
culture, viii, ix, x, xi, 7, 23, 26, 29, 34, 47, 54n2, 68, 75, 83, 121, 122, 129, 153, 154, 157, 163, 179, 198–200, 203, 210, 216, 217, 218n2
customer, vii, 13, 21–3, 29, 31–3, 35n6, 39, 40, 42–9, 52, 54, 63, 64, 67, 74–87, 87n2, 87n3, 110, 113, 114, 117–24, 137, 138, 153, 159, 160, 168–70, 175–8, 184, 185, 187, 189, 190, 197, 198, 205, 208–9, 213, 215, 217
customer-focused behavior, 82–4

customer interaction, 82, 184
customer mistake, 42, 43, 45
customer relationship management (CRM), 82, 208
customer service representative, 42, 82, 169, 187
customer transaction, 43, 169

D

decentralized, 27, 28, 30, 31, 34, 35, 179
decentralized decision-making, 28, 30, 31, 35
decision-making, viii, 28, 30, 31, 35, 38, 44, 71, 98, 109, 110, 115, 130, 160, 168, 179, 180, 191, 206
decision-making processes, 27
Deming, Edward W., 76, 78
differentiation, 17, 60, 137
dissatisfied employee, 127
divergent thinking, 53, 214
diversity, 103, 152, 211
Drucker, Peter, 8, 48, 119
Dyches, Brian, 21

E

Eastern philosophies, 132
economic downturns, 13, 19
effectiveness, 10, 32–3, 35, 95, 138, 164
efficiency, 8, 11, 25, 32–3, 35, 62, 63, 95, 137, 164, 170, 198
emotional connection, 143, 157n2
emotional intelligence, 94, 165, 172
employability, 136, 144, 168, 207, 214

employee development, 90, 94, 209
employees, 4, 5, 7, 9, 13, 14, 18, 27, 29–31, 35, 38, 41, 43, 44, 47–52, 61, 62, 64–72, 75, 80–3, 85, 89–106, 108–10, 112, 114, 115, 120, 122, 123, 125–58, 161, 163–9, 171, 172, 173n, 175–93, 197–217
employment relationship, ix, x, 72n3, 72n5, 87n4, 180, 183, 200, 202, 203, 218n1
empowerment, 27
enablement, 27
engagement survey, 131
enterprise flexibility, 66
enterprising behavior, 44, 49, 91, 186, 188, 190–2, 205, 215
executive leadership, 120, 122
external factors, 5, 13, 19
extrinsic rewards, 43, 49, 85, 125–7, 129, 131, 133, 134, 136, 138, 139, 211

F

facilitator, 188
first-mover advantage, 40
five-year plan, 53, 188
flexibly deployed workforces, 43, 70
flow of information, 177, 179, 188, 191
Ford Motor Company, viii, 61, 177
franchisees, 14
franchising, 13, 50
frontline, 30, 51, 118–21, 184
functional managers, 111–14, 121, 123, 124n2
functional specialization, 44, 76

G

global competition, 132, 169
globalization, 23
global rivalry, 23
goal achievement, 9, 12
goal-driven model, 6–8
goal optimization, 12
goals, 3, 4, 6–15, 17–19, 26, 38, 66, 72n7, 80, 87, 98, 116, 137, 142, 143, 145, 146, 150–1, 156, 157, 165, 172, 181, 184–6, 188, 191, 192, 205, 212, 213, 215
governing bodies, 14
government agencies, 15, 16

H

Hamel, Gary, 137, 140n16, 144, 158n2
Harraf, Abe, 26, 33
Hawthorne studies, 130
head office, 115, 184
hierarchical power, 27, 109, 123
hierarchy, 16, 96, 102, 109, 113, 118, 120, 143, 200
highly skilled employees, 5
high performance culture, viii
high-performing organization, 14–16, 46
human capital, xi
human connectivity, 131
humanists, 128
human motivation, 128
human relation movement, 130
human resources, xi, 10, 11, 110, 112, 158n4, 158n5, 173n2
human resources development (HRD), 10

I

independent thinking, 50, 167
Industrial Revolution, 75, 202
industry standards, 77, 78, 86
information, 23, 25, 27, 31, 42, 79, 82, 85, 97, 103, 109, 160, 169, 172, 175–93, 197, 204, 205, 210, 215–17
information vacuum, 215
initiative, 16, 27, 31, 43, 44, 49–51, 77, 82, 83, 85, 86, 94, 152, 154, 176, 178, 179, 181–93, 193n2, 205, 215, 216
innovation, 5, 23, 26, 34, 40–1, 43–6, 63, 64, 104, 106, 121, 122, 158n6, 180, 181, 207–9, 211
innovation culture, 26
innovation mindset, 26, 64
innovative thinking, 132, 214
inputs, 6, 8–10, 18, 184, 200
intelligence gathering, 17
internal mobility, 61
internal operations, 13, 32
international strategy, 24
interpersonal, 102–4, 109
intrinsic motivation, 127, 134, 136, 139n2, 148, 153, 168, 211, 212, 216, 217n7
investors, 14
iPhone, 40
Ishrak, Omar, 153

J

job boundary, 49
job description, x, 28, 35n8, 41, 44, 49, 61, 68, 86, 89–106, 204, 209

job design, 62–5
job-development, 104
job enlargement, 67, 206
job enrichment, 67, 206
job-holder, 49, 62–4, 70, 90, 93, 94, 97, 162, 164, 165, 172
job rotation, 67, 206
job security, 59, 61, 133
job skills, 66, 94, 96, 106n8, 161, 164, 165, 171, 172
job-specific, 94, 100, 105, 161, 164
job specification, 43, 53, 59–72, 91, 93, 136, 161, 164, 204, 210, 214
judgment, 11, 95, 183, 184, 187, 189, 190, 193n9
Juran, Joseph, 76, 78

K

Kellogg's, 79
key performance indicators (KPIs), 13, 18, 38, 47, 49, 95, 97, 98, 100, 101
key result areas (KRAs), 95, 100, 101
knowledge worker, 128, 130, 139, 177–9, 211
Kodak, 52
KPIs. *See* key performance indicators (KPIs)
KRAs. *See* key result areas (KRAs)

L

large-scale change, 213
leaders, vii, 3, 4, 23, 25, 30, 31, 34, 39, 41, 52, 53, 55n8, 83, 84, 93, 96, 97, 109, 111, 114, 116, 119–23, 128, 137, 138, 140n7, 142, 144–6, 150, 155, 156, 158n6, 162, 166, 168, 170–2, 179, 181–3, 185–92, 200, 206, 217
leadership, 3, 4, 30, 34, 52, 53, 55n8, 83, 96, 97, 109, 116, 120, 122, 182, 206
leadership skills, 109
learning activities, 164, 172
learning organization, 33, 54n2
legislative changes, 13, 19
life skills, 167
linear planning, 53
loyal customers, 85, 213
loyal employee, 138, 141–58, 204, 212, 213

M

management, vii, viii, ix, x, xi, 5, 7, 8, 10, 12, 13, 19n1, 20n5, 26–31, 33, 37, 38, 41, 43, 47–50, 52, 53, 59–87, 89–173, 175–93, 198–208, 210, 217
management by objectives, 8, 19n1
management practices, viii, ix, x, 5, 7, 8, 27–9, 47, 48, 53, 67, 90–2, 99, 128, 135, 178, 192, 199
managerial strategies, viii, ix, x, 5, 7, 8, 13, 27–9, 33, 47, 48, 53, 62, 65, 67, 70, 71, 90–2, 99, 123, 128, 134, 135, 178, 192, 199
marketing, 12, 24, 47, 61, 69, 79, 108, 110, 112, 114, 116, 124n5, 139n2, 140n3

marketing gurus, 61
marketplace, 5, 6, 11, 18, 22, 23, 28, 32, 34, 35, 39, 40, 52–4, 59, 65, 71, 80, 94, 105, 111, 123, 133, 145, 161, 162, 192, 208, 211
market research, 17
Maslow, Abraham, 133
McDonalds, 13, 50, 63, 64
Medtronic, 152, 153
meetings, 3, 42, 46, 74, 77, 78, 84, 86, 104, 107, 108, 152, 160, 185, 186, 188, 193, 200, 201, 203
mentoring, 122, 187, 192
Meyer, John, 147–9, 157, 158n4
micro-management, 77
Microsoft, 24
military, 16, 24, 25, 109, 189, 190
mission, 25, 113, 130, 144, 147, 153, 156, 188
monetary incentives, 130, 133, 139
Moss Kanter, Rosabeth, viii, 38, 54
multi-dimensional, 160, 162, 163, 170–2, 205, 213, 214
multi-dimensional learning, 162, 170, 214
multidimensional strategy, 162
multi-disciplinary teams, 44
multi-skilling, 65–8, 70–2, 206, 207

N

networks, 14, 25, 179
new capitalism, 132
new working arrangement, 145
niche market, 60, 61, 71
non-job roles, 90, 91, 93, 95, 96, 99–106, 122, 170, 205, 209, 216

non-technical capabilities, 93, 160
non-technical development, 161, 178
not-for-profit enterprise, 8
not-for-profit sector, 138

O

on-boarding, 93
open dialogue, 180, 216
open system, 6, 19, 20n7
operational decisions, 184
operations, 3, 13, 21, 24, 32, 33, 35, 46, 48, 62, 63, 75, 78, 97, 104, 107, 110, 112, 114, 116, 118–22, 166, 183, 184, 187, 188
organizational agility model, viii, 34, 38, 39, 44, 45, 53, 54, 60, 168, 206
organizational ambidexterity, 17, 18, 20n5
organizational behavior, 8, 34
organizational culture, ix, 29, 203, 216, 217
organizational direction, 179
organizational hierarchy, 96, 109
organizational improvement, 5, 209
organizational learning, 33–4, 54n2
organizational restructuring, 131
organizational speed, viii
organizational structure, viii, 17, 33, 35, 102, 107, 116–18, 120, 124n4, 124n5, 179
organizational success, viii, 11, 19, 25, 101
organizational values, 152–3, 157
organization development, x, 8, 10, 104

organizing structures, x, 32, 33, 108–10, 113, 115, 118–20, 210, 216
outputs, 5, 6, 8–10, 12, 46, 103, 104
ownership, 151, 169, 183, 197, 212

P

paramilitary, 16
partnerships, 23
Pavlovian conditioning, 49
pay levels, 95
peer relationships, 152
people management practices, x, 5, 7, 8, 27, 28, 33, 47, 48, 53, 62, 65, 67, 70, 71, 90, 99
performance benefits, 155
performance evaluation, 5, 8, 19
performance feedback, 156, 186, 192
performance management, vii, viii, ix, x, xi, 8, 10, 13, 29, 41, 49, 53, 91, 92, 100, 123, 127, 128, 134, 135, 160, 178, 179, 191, 192, 199, 206, 207
performance management practices, viii, ix, 13, 29, 91, 92, 123, 128, 134, 135, 178, 192, 199
performance management system, 100
performance-oriented enterprise, 167
performance review, x, 41, 54n4, 92, 97–100, 106, 173n4
performance review interview, 97, 106
personal goals, 150
personal objectives, 146, 156, 157

personal productivity, 127
Pink, Dan H., 128, 134–8, 140n8, 140n11, 140n13, 140n19, 212
plans-of-action, 188
polar opposite, 16, 17, 23, 81, 97, 192, 203
policy making, 184
poor performance, 14, 159, 160, 171
poor-performing teams, 162
positive energy, 209
power, 15, 27, 28, 30, 34, 109, 112, 113, 123n2, 123n6, 124n2, 137, 200
power-bases, 15
prescriptive approach, 214
pressure groups, 14
PricewaterhouseCoopers, 79
problem-based learning, 162, 169
problem-solving, 16, 45, 50–2, 54, 160, 167–72, 189, 193, 207, 211
problem-solving capabilities, 168
procedural knowledge, 94, 161, 167
procedure-driven environment, 64
procedures manual, 51
process control, 75, 76
process development, 13
process-driven industries, 50
process model, 6, 12–14, 19, 77, 80
product inspection, 76
production, 9, 12, 67, 69, 75, 77, 104, 114, 120, 137, 138, 159, 165, 180, 198
product life cycles, 40
product line, 12, 113–15, 117, 124
product quality, 75, 114
product team, 113
professional goals, 150, 188

profit, viii, 3–20, 23, 24, 38, 40, 47, 138, 147, 179, 181, 198, 207, 211
profit margins, viii, 7, 198
project manager, 108, 109, 112, 113, 119, 121, 123, 124n2
project teams, 31, 32, 35, 44, 83, 103, 108, 111, 114, 119–23, 135, 136, 205, 211
promotional opportunities, 96
psychological contract, ix, x, 145, 156, 158n3, 197–218

Q

quality assurance, 6, 13, 76, 79

R

recruitment and selection, 91–3, 121
regular dialogue, 150, 186
regulation, 14, 16, 189, 215
regulators, 14, 77, 86
remuneration, 92, 95–6, 105
resource constraints, 5
retail design institute, 21
retailers, 21, 23
retail outlet, 85, 183, 184
retention, 85, 153, 180
retirement, 89, 90, 132, 144
retirement plan, 144
rewards and incentives, 70, 121, 128
risk-adverse, 215
roadmap, 34
role clarity, 82
role description, 91, 100, 101, 105, 205
roles and responsibilities, 75, 110, 187

S

safety standards, 187
salesperson, 43, 81, 85, 140n3
satisfied employee, 125–40, 212
school of thought, 8, 12, 16, 18, 170
scientific management, viii, ix, 50, 53, 60, 62–5, 71, 74–7, 86, 90, 108, 110, 128–30, 160–2, 178, 191, 192, 198, 199, 202, 203
secondment, 207
Seet, Daniel, 112, 124n2
selection process, 92, 93, 105
self-actualization, 133
self-development, 104, 165, 171
self-direction, 135, 136
self-discovery, 167
self-improvement, 212
self-mastery, 130, 212
self-sufficiency, 128, 134
Senge, Peter, 33
senior management, 107, 118, 122
Setili, Amanda, 24, 35n3
Sinek, Simon, 137, 140n18
skill development, 11, 66, 160–2, 171
skill mastery, 95, 164
skills-sets, 47, 60–2, 65, 89, 92, 94, 96, 115, 117, 144, 148, 169, 177, 178, 211
S.M.A.R.T. goals, 9
smartphone, 24, 46, 79
social media, 177
socio-economic trends, 13, 19
Soloman, Micah, 79
specialization, ix, 27, 44, 47, 60–7, 70–2, 76, 83, 90, 94, 105, 110, 111, 123, 136, 161, 207, 210

specialized skills-set, 61
speed, viii, ix, x, 5, 6, 13, 22, 23, 25, 26, 30, 38–45, 48, 54, 62, 64, 93, 114, 116, 124, 187, 207–11, 214
stakeholder model, 14–16, 19, 32
stakeholders, 6, 12, 14–16, 19, 23, 25, 31, 32, 35, 38, 46, 78, 92, 106, 114, 159, 160
statistical quality control, 76
strategic direction, 29–30, 34, 52, 122, 150, 156
strategic plan, 23, 52, 53
strategic planning, 8, 53, 188, 189, 193
strengths, 7, 15, 109, 150, 151, 163, 169, 170, 172, 214
structural fluidity, 33
substandard performance, 159, 170, 171
subsystems, 10–13
succession plan, 96
supervision, 69, 115
suppliers, 7, 12, 180
supply chains, 33, 78
sustainability, 5, 15
systems model, 6, 10–13, 19, 47, 83
systems thinking, 10–13, 15, 19, 47

T

talent, 85, 96, 112, 146, 151, 180, 214, 216
talent management, 96
Taylor, Frederick, viii, 62, 63, 71, 72n2, 75–7, 86, 94, 95, 108, 129, 130, 140n10, 144
Taylorism, viii, ix, 60, 62, 63, 72n2, 75, 76, 163, 164, 172

team development, 94, 160
team meetings, 186
technical skill, 93, 94, 105, 115, 160–2, 172
technological innovation, 23
throughputs, 6, 9, 10, 18
top talent, 146, 180
total quality control, 76
total quality management, 76
trainee, 161, 167, 214
training programs, 41, 66–8, 89, 94, 160, 163–7, 171, 172
train the trainer, 70
transfer, 71, 207
trust, 4, 160, 176, 187–9, 201
tunnel vision, 65

U

Ulrich, Dave, 128, 137, 140n7
Ulrich, Wendy, 128, 137, 140n7
unethical behavior, 191, 193
unions, 14, 176
United Kingdom, 24, 66, 67
United States of America (USA), 24

V

value-sets, 16, 17
vested interest, 14, 15, 115
vision, 29, 30, 33, 34, 60, 65, 119, 122, 149, 166, 188
vision statement, 29
VUCA, 94, 104, 111, 123, 180

W

waste minimization, 62
website, 42, 74, 181

Western society, 130–3, 139
whole-of-enterprise approach, 47
work environment, 9, 47, 50, 109, 129
worker mobility, 155
working relationships, ix, x, 27, 96, 143, 152, 156, 157, 176, 199–201, 203, 213
work-life balance, 153–7
work motivation, 127
workplace community, 131
workplace culture, x, 121, 198–200
workplace investigations, 191, 193
World War II, 76

Printed by Printforce, the Netherlands